EVERY MAN HAS HIS PRICE

EVERY MAN HAS HIS PRICE

THE TRUE STORY OF WRESTLING'S MILLION DOLLAR MAN

BY TED DiBIASE

MULTNOMAH PUBLISHERS

Sisters, Oregon

EVERY MAN HAS HIS PRICE
published by Multnomah Publishers, Inc.
© 1997 by Ted DiBiase

In association with Wolgemuth & Hyatt, Inc.,
8012 Brooks Chapel Road, Brentwood, TN 37027

International Standard Book Number: 1-57673-175-8
Printed in the United States of America

Cover design by Jeff Gelfuso

Scripture quotations are from the *New American Standard Bible* (NASB)
© 1960, 1977 by the Lockman Foundation

For information:
MULTNOMAH PUBLISHERS, INC.
Post Office Box 1720
Sisters, Oregon 97759

Library of Congress Cataloging-in-Publication Data
DiBiase, Ted.
    Every man has his price/by Ted DiBiase.
        p. cm.
    ISBN 1-57673-175-8 (alk. paper)
    1. DiBiase, Ted. 2. Christian biography—United States. 3. Wrestlers—United States—
Biography. 4. World Wrestling Federation—Biography. I. Title.
BR1725.D53A3   1997
277.3'082'092—dc21   97-14403
    [B]   CIP

98 99 00 01 02 03 04 — 10 9 8 7 6 5 4 3 2

I would like to dedicate this book to my wife, Melanie, and my three sons, Michael, Teddy, and Brett. Mel, you have stood by me in the most difficult of times and given me the greatest treasures of my life, my sons. And, boys, you, along with Mom, are truly the greatest gifts God has ever given me. I am so blessed.

Table of Contents

ACKNOWLEDGMENTS

I first wish to thank Rendy Lovelady for encouraging me to pursue the writing of this book and for leading me to Robert Wolgemuth. Robert, I thank you for having faith in this project. Without you it would have never happened. I would also like to thank Joe Lovelady for his guidance throughout this project. Then, of course, I thank you, Bill Butterworth, for doing a wonderful job of helping me to tell my story. And last, but certainly not least, I thank my Lord and Savior, Jesus Christ. For without Him I am nothing, and through Him I can do anything (Philippians 4:13).

1
THE WORLD CHAMPION!
THE MILLION DOLLAR MAN!

It was the biggest moment of my wrestling career.

With my bodyguard, Virgil, at my side, I hustled out of my limo, signed autographs, and entered a service entrance leading to a tangle of catacombs beneath Market Square Arena in Indianapolis on a crisp Saturday afternoon in the autumn of 1987. The big draw that night was a rematch between Hulk Hogan and Andre the Giant for the world championship—with a special appearance by the Million Dollar Man. For the thousands of fans of professional wrestling, it was the sort of main event that defines the phrase, "It doesn't get any better than this!"

Just six months before, there had been a title match between Hulk and Andre that marked the beginning of this intense rivalry. They had been friends, but in this match Andre turned from his normal "good guy" image to an enemy of Hogan's. The victory went to Hulk, which was no small task because, even though Hulk is six feet eight inches tall and weighs 300 pounds, he defeated a man who stood seven feet four inches tall and weighed 450 pounds. Andre was a true giant!

And it was not an event observed by only a few die-hard fans either. Hulk defeated Andre at Wrestlemania III, which was held near Detroit at the Pontiac Silverdome. The world record for attendance at an indoor event was set that March night in Pontiac, as more than 93,000 people were in attendance as these two went at it in the evening's main event.

But tonight's event wasn't just about Hulk Hogan and Andre the Giant. There was a third party who had entered this story line, who threatened to claim the championship belt as his own—without even entering the ring.

Who would have the arrogance to lay hold of the title without wrestling for it? Who would be so vain? Who? The most evil villain the world of wrestling has ever seen: the Million Dollar Man. And that's me, Ted DiBiase.

I made my mark in the world of professional wrestling living by the motto *Every Man Has His Price.* The Million Dollar Man could buy anything and anybody. And now, because Hulk Hogan was at one of his highest peaks of popularity, I decided to go after him with gusto.

"Hulk Hogan, I can buy you!" I would taunt him during one of our many prematch video promotions.

"No you can't!" he'd scream back with his typical intensity. "I can't be bought!"

"Well, if I can't buy you, then I'll just have to buy the World Wrestling Federation title!" I bellowed in my most evil voice.

"How are you going to do that?" he prodded.

"You'll see. Every man has his price," I said with a knowing smile, for I had an evil plan up my sleeve.

With that setup, I approached the championship evening. In many ways it was an out-of-the-ordinary event, but in other ways it was just another venue.

PREPARING FOR THE SHOW

The wrestlers arrive as early as noon for a 7:00 P.M. event. We warmly greet one another as we wander the halls that surround the auditorium. The corridors are now busy with a crew of guys all dressed in dark blue jumpsuits with the WWF logo printed on their backs in large yellow letters. They are bringing in the ring, piece by piece, from one of the WWF tractor-trailer rigs that travel from town to town. Other members of the crew hang from rafters, climb cherry-pickers, and man scaffolds as they painstakingly set up floodlights, lasers, and some of the many special effects that all contribute to a night of wrestling. A sound crew checks over the sound system for any possible glitches. Still others are scurrying around with T-shirts that read "NBC Sports" on the front, because this event will be televised nationally as part of NBC's Saturday night wrestling program. Large cameras are placed in their positions, monitors are set up in strategic locations, and young men with minicams strapped to their shoulders get the feel of ringside as they ready themselves for the "no mistakes allowed" world of a live, national broadcast.

Outside the auditorium but still inside the arena, remote sets are constructed for the many video interviews that take place during an event like this one. Producers with clipboards run around asking a thousand questions, attempting to put everything in order for the show.

Farther down the hall are sections roped off for the makeup crew. Tables, chairs, stools, and carts all seem to be overflowing with enough makeup to fill another truck. Makeup is an important part of our traveling production company, both for a character like mine, who only needs to take the shine off his face under the bright lights of the arena, and for some of wrestling's more exotic performers like the Ultimate Warrior, whose painted face is a cross between a punk rock star and a native American in a cowboys-and-Indians movie.

A few steps farther back, we enter the area set aside for wardrobe. Here are costumes of every color and style hanging from wire hangers, draped over tables, wadded up in large piles, and sitting peacefully in the large trunks we use to transport them from stop to stop. Two young girls are doing the work of fifteen seamstresses as they hem pant legs on a pair of Spandex wrestling shorts, let out the waist for a wrestler who's been eating too well lately, press the wrinkles out of a costume, and sew on buttons that have gone astray.

The wrestlers themselves have all been assigned dressing rooms for this evening's performance. A guy like Hulk gets his own dressing room, but most of the others share less-glamorous facilities. But no one is to be found in the dressing rooms at this time of day, for it's still too early.

We're all in a room that has been taken over by the caterers. Long, narrow silver trays sit above warmers on white-linen-covered tables as we line up one after another for salad, rolls, pasta with marinara sauce, and broiled chicken breasts. (There is a sign posted above the chicken that reads "For Wrestlers Only," which brings a few jokes in our direction from the rest of the crew.) Top it all off with a piece of chocolate layer cake and a Diet Coke, and the meal is complete. The room is fairly large, and it is set up with six or seven long tables that each seats about two dozen folks. We end up eating in small groups of four or five, talking quietly about everything from the weather, to the best hotel rates in this town, to who will be at Madison Square Garden the next time we wrestle in New York City.

We're all a big family. Wrestlers eat with tech-crew members, promoters chat with managers, producers cut up with agents. To see us in this setting, you'd never know that in a few short hours we'll be at each other's throats.

The wrestlers are all dressed casually in sweatpants, tennis shoes, and sweat-shirts advertising everything from the WWF to Gold's Gym to the Chicago Bulls. One guy is wearing a shirt that simply reads "John 3:16."

The consistent thing about the shirts we wear is that most of us cut off the sleeves to give us more room to move around and to show off the biceps we've been working on. After our meal, everyone scatters, preparing for his part in tonight's program in his own individual way. Most of the guys head for the dressing rooms to put on their costumes for the evening. Entering my dressing area, I can't help but stare at the black suit with the shiny gold dollar signs on the lapels that hangs next to the freshly pressed white tuxedo shirt in my locker. Wearing that outfit will transform me into a character who can incite a crowd to riot against me. Even my family and friends can't believe how evil I can be. I chuckle as I think to myself, *And wait until they see what I have up my sleeve for tonight's championship match!*

I'm psyched, so I pace a lot in my little area as I attempt to walk off some of my nervous energy. On the other end of the spectrum is Andre the Giant. Tucked away in a corner of the dressing room, he is quietly playing cards, appearing not to have a worry in the world. A seasoned veteran, Andre instructs me in his heavy French accent, "Let me know when it's time to go out, kid," as he goes on with his game.

The pungent odor of Ben Gay tells everyone that a wrestler has a sore muscle that once again will be tested to its limits tonight in the ring. Backstage, the smell of liniment gives way to the smell of cigar smoke. Many of the previous generation of wrestlers are still an active part of this business. Legends like Gorilla Monsoon and Killer Kowalski are distracted from their card game by a few last-minute changes that need to be explained to the crew, as some of their peers puff on stogies and wait for the next deal of the cards.

INTRODUCING THE MILLION DOLLAR MAN

The relatively quiet time of endless waiting yields to the stressful final few minutes before we make our triumphant entrances. Andre is summoned from his dressing room, as is Hulk.

It's Match Time! The main event is announced over the public address system, and the adrenaline starts pumping by the gallon. We stand behind the black velvet curtain that separates us from the screaming fans. One by one, we are announced over the arena's loudspeaker, and we make our entrances as our theme songs crank up to a head-pounding volume. Hulk and Andre are cheered and jeered in a frenzied mixture, but when I pass through the curtain, it's a solid chorus of "boo's." Judging from the crowd response, I'm a better villain than I realized.

Over the past few months I was a part of so many video vignettes introducing my character to the public that I should have known how easily I could disgust a crowd. Here are a few of my favorite features:

One starts with a clip that shows me riding in a stretch limousine. "Hello, I'm Ted DiBiase, and I'm the Million Dollar Man," I say to the camera. "I can buy *anything,*" I emphasize over and over. In this particular clip, I'm counting a wad of money thicker than most folks would see in their entire lives. In the midst of adding up all my dough, I cut my finger on a fresh $100 bill. I turn to my faithful bodyguard, saying, "I need a doctor, Virgil. Take me to one immediately."

The next scene is a doctor's waiting room filled with people. "I need to see the doctor right now," I instruct the nurse at the receptionist's station.

"I'm sorry, but all these people are ahead of you. They all need to see the doctor too," she answers curtly.

"I don't think you understand," I reply calmly as I reach into my pocket, grab my money roll, and start peeling off $100 bills one by one. "I need to see the doctor *now.*"

She is taken aback at the amount of money that is being thrown her way. Before too long, I have made my point. The vignette ends with me being ushered into the doctor's office ahead of everyone else in the waiting room. I turn to the camera, grinning with sheer evil and slyly conclude, "You see, *everybody* has a price for the Million Dollar Man!"

Another vignette we filmed was staged at a four-star restaurant. The crowd in the front suggests that there is quite a wait to get in. But as my limousine pulls up, I get out and bark at the maître d', "I want a table!"

"Sir, there is at least a twenty-minute wait," he apologizes.

"You don't understand, my good man. I don't wait," I calmly reply as I start throwing C-notes his way. "I don't wait for *anything!*"

And, of course, shortly I am being escorted to my table.

"Don't be upset with this man," I tell the camera as I confidently stride to my table. "For, you see, *every man* has his price!"

Then there was the time I was at a hotel, asking for the very best room in the place. "That would be the honeymoon suite sir," the front desk attendant explains to me.

"That will be fine," I say.

"But sir, it is already occupied," he answers nervously, sensing the anger this would produce.

"Well, is that going to be a big problem?" I calmly reply, turning to my trusty wad of cash. As I unfold more $100 bills, the man at the front desk begins to see things my way. The clip concludes with us evicting a couple of newlyweds.

Another vignette involves the Million Dollar Man driving up to a public pool. Before the skit is over, the facility is transformed into my own private pool. After all the kids are tossed out of the pool, and the pool attendant's fists are full of money, I say to him, "I think the chlorine level is too high, don't you agree?" He immediately goes about adjusting the levels.

We kept producing more and more of these vignettes to further fuel the fans' anger. I'd go to an arena and pay some poor, unsuspecting young lady as much as $300 to bark like a dog. But it wasn't just the barking; it was making her get down on her hands and knees that completed the picture of humiliation. "You see, *every one* has a price for the Million Dollar Man!" I'd gush for the camera.

The Million Dollar Man's biggest attention-getter took place in the Mecca Arena in Milwaukee, Wisconsin. I find a five-year-old boy who is as cute as a button.

"Can you bounce a basketball?" I ask the eager young child.

"Yes!" he replies excitedly.

"Can you bounce it ten times in a row?"

"Uh-huh," he answers.

I take him up to the podium, and he shows the crowd he is true to his word, dribbling the ball ten straight times.

"That's great," I say. "Now, if you can bounce the ball *fifteen* times in a row, I'll give you $500."

The crowd cheers its approval as the boy begins the simple task of making big money.

But in an act as dastardly as any I have ever done, when the boy finishes his fourteenth dribble, I stick out my foot, causing him to miss the last bounce. The crowd gasps in disbelief, then boos me in an angry chorus.

"When you don't get the job done, you don't get the money!" I scream to the arena.

At this point, the little boy is so crushed that he sticks his thumb in his mouth, starts to cry, and runs to his mother's waiting arms. It is the Million Dollar Man at his most evil!

(I should hasten to explain that we had preselected this child, and we had agreed to give him the money if he just played along with the gag. By the time we filmed it, he apparently had forgotten our deal, for he was genuinely upset. I still have people who ask about that particular vignette. But, yes, the kid got the money!)

These were the sorts of things that were a part of the character known as the Million Dollar Man. I was given $2,000 worth of $100 bills as often as I needed it. The instructions were to throw that money around as freely as I could. Every time I bought so much as a pack of gum or a newspaper, I paid for it with a $100 bill. That was the drill, and one in which I gleefully participated. It was a blast!

SHOWTIME!

Back at Market Square Arena's ringside, the hammer strikes the bell, signifying the match has begun. You don't have to hang around wrestling for long to realize the value of the shock factor. Part of what keeps people's interest week after week is not knowing what will take place in any given match.

In this particular bout, Hulk dominates from the start. I'm fussing and fuming at ringside, slamming my hands on the ring's canvas floor, pleading with Andre to rebound in order to put the Hulkster in his place. In my plan, it is absolutely vital for Andre to be the victor.

As things continue to go Hulk's way, it just seems like the time is right for something unexpected to happen. In a move that brings a resounding groan from the crowd, the referee, Dave Hebner, becomes tangled between the two wrestlers and is knocked out cold. With Dave sprawled out on the floor of the ring, I pounce into action. Grabbing him by his two ankles, I drag his unconscious body out of the ring and give the sign for what is to happen next.

To the utter shock of everybody, a new referee appears from the shadows and takes command of the match. What makes the switch especially exciting is that the new referee is Dave Hebner's identical twin brother, Earl. But, thanks to the influence of the Million Dollar Man, Earl is Dave's evil twin.

Andre knows what this is all about, so he grabs Hulk, lifting him high above his head, and throws him to the canvas. Andre jumps on Hulk, setting up the pin. But Hulk has only one shoulder touching the mat, not the two that are required. Don't forget, Earl is the evil twin. I guess Earl doesn't have a very good angle to observe the situation, because he counts, "One...two...three" and slams his right hand down on the mat, signifying the pin for Andre's victory and Hulk's defeat!

The crowd goes ballistic! Hulk protests that he only had one shoulder down, but Earl won't hear of it. The huge, gold championship belt is awarded to Andre the Giant, and this is my cue to enter the ring. Boldly, proudly, with all the arrogance I can muster, I stride over to Andre. He presents me with the belt he has just won. As I hoist the prize over my head, the world knows what has just taken place. *I bought off Andre to give me the belt once he won it!*

By now Hulk is about to explode in anger and frustration. Dave Hebner has regained consciousness at ringside, so Hulk yanks him back into the ring. To the delight of the television cameraman right in front of him, Hulk has a twin in each hand. He looks to his right at Dave, looks to his left at Earl, and then stares straight into the camera with a shaken look of disbelief.

Andre and I have left the ring at this point. It's a good thing we did too. In complete exasperation, Hulk sends evil twin Earl Hebner flying out of the ring with one mighty toss. Fortunately, Andre and I catch Earl, so no damage is done. We all just grin like three cats who have swallowed canaries as we know we have won the championship through the sheer genius of the Million Dollar Man's dastardly deeds. This is really fun!

A WILD RIDE TO THE TOP

It was a night filled with emotion for me. As I sat in the dressing room, staring at the championship belt that was now mine, I began changing out of my wrestling gear and back into my street clothes. I was leaving the Million Dollar Man in a locker. Returning to the private world of Ted DiBiase, my mind was overflowing with nostalgia.

I thought of all those years I had wrestled in comparative obscurity, only dreaming of a night like tonight. I thought of my sweet wife, Melanie, and Michael, Teddy, and Brett, my three fantastic sons. I thought about how faithful and supportive they have been of me in this crazy business that I love.

I also thought about my dad, "Iron Mike" DiBiase. I thought of all the years he had wrestled as a part of the generation that preceded mine. Thinking back on all I learned from this incredibly special man, I found myself thinking about how he never wanted me to wrestle but how proud he would be tonight. I thought to myself, *If my dad could see all this, how big this business has become...if he could've seen me in the ring holding high the championship belt...if only Iron Mike could gaze at the enormous world of the WWF, he would be so proud of me.*

Thoughts of Iron Mike caused me to think of my mom and my brothers and a host of other people who were significant in my life. But most of all, I thought of another very important person in my life. My mother's mother had taken me and raised me as one of her own when I was just a small child. My grandmother had worked hard all her life, and in doing so she instilled in me the faith and the values that I carry with me even as I write these words.

From the desolate plains of cactus in the high desert to the glitz and glamour of the WWF, that night I realized I'd come a long way from the humble beginnings in southern Arizona.

It's been one wild ride!

2
MARIE'S TRUCK STOP CAFE

In the sleepy little town of Willcox, Arizona, I don't think many of the towns-people would recognize the name of Verda Marie Nevins if I were to mention it. But if I were to say Marie from over at Marie's Truck Stop Cafe, the whole town would smile in recognition.

I can close my eyes and still hear the folks making their comments about her:

"She's the nicest lady in town—no question about it!"

"Marie would do anything for you, and I mean anything! She's the most giving person I've ever met."

"If you were down on your luck and needed a hot meal, Marie would make sure you were fed, no questions asked. That's just the kind of person she is. Really caring and compassionate."

"If you're on the road and you're looking for good food, look for the place with all the big rigs parked in front of it. Truckers know where the best food in town is located. In these parts, all the truckers eat at Marie's. Her donuts are out of this world!"

"Marie bakes all her own pastries, and let me assure you, they are the best homemade pastries for miles!"

"There's much more to Marie than just liking people. She genuinely cares for them."

That's Marie from Marie's Truck Stop Cafe in Willcox, Arizona. She's the lady named Verda Marie Nevins. She's my grandmother. But Willcox is getting a little ahead in my story.

THE ROAD TO WILLCOX

Our family didn't start out in Arizona. Both my parents' families grew up in Omaha, Nebraska. What's amazing is that my father used to deliver papers to my mother's house on his morning paper route, yet they never met until years later out on the road.

My mother, Helen, grew up in the home of her parents, Edgar and Marie

Nevins. Even in Omaha, Grandma ran a restaurant down on Leavenworth Avenue. My grandfather was an engineer for the Union Pacific Railroad, so he would be gone for long stretches of time, riding the rails all over the United States. Grandma worked hard, running the restaurant virtually by herself. And if you know anything about the restaurant business, you know how demanding it is.

In the midst of all this busyness, my mother was born in 1927. She was a pretty little girl, gregarious and a real free spirit. She was a bit more than Grandma and Grandpa could handle, especially with the long hours they were keeping on their respective jobs. Thus, my mother really raised herself, and as a result she learned the ways of the world very quickly. In 1943, at sixteen years of age, my mother married a wrestler named Al Galento. Shortly after, they had a son, whom they named Michael. Then, to complete this whirlwind period of my mother's life, she divorced Al when she discovered he was already running around on her. Sixteen, married, a mother, a divorcée. She was too young for all this to be happening.

Because she had an exceptional talent for dancing, my mother was hired as a showgirl. She started traveling with shows that toured all over the country. She was part of a troupe that would open for or back up people like Frank Sinatra and the famous Big Bands of the 1940s. It was a terrific break for my mother, who had already experienced more than her share of pain.

It was obvious that my mother could not travel with an infant son, so the child-rearing responsibilities fell to my grandparents, specifically my grandmother. She took this charge seriously. Things were tight for my grandparents in Omaha, and their lives were further complicated by the stigma of having a divorced daughter with a baby boy. My grandmother, a free spirit herself, decided to take matters into her own hands.

One day, Grandma read an advertisement announcing an opportunity to run a cafe in a small town in Arizona. Right then and there she decided what she needed to do. She explained her decision to her husband, packed a few things, bundled up baby Michael, and bought a ticket on a Greyhound bus to Willcox. She answered the ad in person and immediately completed the transaction giving her ownership of what was to become Marie's Truck Stop Cafe.

HELEN AND TED—AND ME

Grandma's decision to leave Omaha was a huge one for my grandparents, but it had little effect on my mother, who was on the road just about all the time.

There was an event right around this time, however, that would have an impact on her life. While she was out on the road touring, she met a handsome young singer, with a beautiful bass voice, by the name of Ted Wills. He was a dashing young man from West Palm Beach, Florida, and he swept Helen off her feet.

They fell in love, and before long, they were married.

Ted Wills and Helen Nevins were my father and mother. I was born on January 18, 1954, in Miami, Florida.

Unfortunately, I didn't get much of a chance to build a life with my folks, especially my dad. Being in the world of nightclubs, part of my parents' normal lifestyle was to attend plenty of parties. They both started drinking, which especially affected my mother. She desperately wanted to feel a sense of security, but Ted was not providing it for her. It was more than she could handle, so shortly after I was born, my mother and father divorced.

Years later, I asked my mother why she divorced my dad. "It wasn't that Ted was a bad guy," Mom began. "I mean, he didn't beat me or anything like that. But I so wanted to feel secure. Ted didn't meet that need for me."

I nodded my head, trying to understand.

Then she added, "He had talent but no ambition. He was the kind of guy who would sit back waiting for the big break to come to him, rather than going out looking to make it happen. He was just too carefree for me."

Besides the normal stress a divorce would put on a family, we had another set of issues to deal with. I was just a baby, and Mom had already learned that the road was no place for babies. Where was I going to live? My mom was still making her living on the circuit, so I needed a place to go.... Marie's Truck Stop Cafe.

HOME...TO GRANDMA

Willcox, Arizona, is one of those dust-blown towns out in the middle of nowhere. Not only did it have just one stoplight, it had only one street that was covered with blacktop. The main street in town was paved, but all the other avenues were dirt roads, complete with ruts, rocks, stones, and dust.

The year was 1956, yet I can distinctly recall thoughts and feelings that were right out of the '20s and '30s. I remember friends of mine who were growing up in homes without indoor plumbing. I had other friends who had no running water. The Baby Boom was in full swing, President Eisenhower was overseeing incredible progress in our post-World War II America, yet I hung out with kids who still had outhouses and outside, hand-cranked water pumps.

Nestled in the plains of the high desert, Willcox is located about eighty miles outside of Tucson. When I lived there, I would estimate the town's population was no more than five or six thousand people. It was quite an experience to grow up in that town at that time, because it was still possible to discover traces of the Old West. We lived near the historic town of Tombstone and the national forest where Cochise, the Apache chief, is buried, although part of the historical tradition insists that no one knows exactly where his remains are located in that forest. Our tiny town was just discovering television, where they were immortalizing our area through westerns like *Wyatt Earp* and *Have Gun, Will Travel.*

My grandmother accepted me with love and affection when my mom brought me to her modest home. She was already raising my older brother, Michael, so she was used to the regimen of being in charge of a youngster. Their cozy two-bedroom home was now full—Grandma and Grandpa sharing one bedroom, Michael and I sharing the other one (although as soon as I was old enough to get around, I used to love to crawl in my grandparents' bed!). Being eight years younger than he was, I'm sure I was a real trial for Mike, but he didn't have much of a choice.

We really didn't spend all that much time at the house. Most of my early years revolved around the day-to-day routine at Marie's Truck Stop Cafe. My grandmother typically worked a shift of 6 A.M. to 2 P.M., but because it was her cafe, there were plenty of days where she would be pulling double shifts, working from six in the morning all the way through to midnight.

The truck stop attracted a wide variety of clientele. Obviously, there were lots of long-haul truck drivers who would plan their itineraries to include a stop at Marie's for a meal. But there were many other ways of life represented in the booths and at the counter of that restaurant.

A large part of the Willcox economy was tied up in agriculture, specifically the raising of lettuce. I can still recall the migrant workers who would be brought in, especially at harvest time to pick the ripe crop. The farmers would be at the front door of the cafe as soon as the doors opened in the morning, requesting that my grandmother put together as many boxes of freshly baked donuts as she could. They were delicious and fairly inexpensive, so the farmers saw them as the perfect food to feed the migrant workers who were working the fields.

Grandma never turned away anyone. Several hundred yards behind the back door of the cafe was a set of railroad tracks. Long, winding chains of dirty brown freight cars were a common sight, their wheels slowly but deliberately grinding on the rails with the sounds of steel on steel. Many nights we would hear the persistent pounding of a fist on the back door of the cafe after the final car had faded into the horizon. Upon answering it, we would discover what we used to call a hobo—someone who was unemployed and down on his luck wandering the countryside by sneaking rides in an empty box car. Marie saw to it that not one of them was ever turned away hungry. I learned a great deal about compassion by watching my grandmother.

The local townsfolk used to love to eat at the truck stop as well. One of my earliest childhood memories is meeting up with an older man from down the road whose wife had died. Everyone called him Smitty. The widower took all his meals at the cafe. Smitty and I became good friends, always striking up a conversation whenever we saw one another.

By trade, Smitty was an upholsterer. I recall the day he invited me to his workshop so I could watch him perform his craft. I sat awestruck as he held a couple of dozen tacks in his mouth. One by one, he would spit them out onto his hammer, which had a magnetic head. With expert precision, he would pop out those tacks like a machine gun firing. He'd hammer each one in an exact row, completing his job.

One day he surprised me by asking, "Teddy, would you like to try your hand at upholstering?"

"Can I?" I asked, my eyes as wide as beach balls.

"If it's OK with your grandmother, it's sure all right with me. You've been watching me long enough to know what you're doing!"

I checked with Grandma, who said it was all right but quickly reminded me to be careful.

"I'll be careful, Grandma!" I shouted, already out the front door and heading down the road.

The widower set me up with an old piece of lumber, some remnants of material, a hammer, and some tacks. Having watched him as closely as I had, I knew the drill. Looking back, I'm not sure how handsome that rough piece of lumber looked with the tattered piece of upholstery on it, but I do remember how proud I was of my accomplishment.

Yes, at three years old, I was already an expert upholsterer, not to mention knowing all there was to know about climbing up onto a stool at the cafe's counter and drinking a cup of coffee with my friends, the truckers. I must have provided hours of entertainment for them, trying so hard to act grown up. But in all those hours listening to them spin yarns, I sure learned how to tell a story!

I loved to hear those guys tell their tales, but even more, I loved going to the movies. I can remember Grandma placing two quarters in my sweaty little palm, instructing me to ride my bike down to the movie house for the Saturday matinee. Today, my sons sit in amazement when I explain to them that back then with fifty cents, not only could I get into the movie, (that was only a quarter), but I also had ten cents for popcorn, ten cents for a soda, and a nickel for a candy bar.

And to top it all off, I was doing these things all by myself, riding my bike all over town, all before I even entered the first grade!

A Woman of Tenderness, Toughness, and Compassion

My grandmother was a very loving woman, but she was also very tough. She had an inner strength that helped her through some difficult times. I'm not really certain if Grandma was a Christian at this point, because she didn't begin talking about her faith until later in my childhood. But I do know that she operated by a set of core values that were very Christlike in nature.

For example, when I was still a toddler, a frightening day arrived where there was a grease fire in the back of the restaurant that set the entire place ablaze. Grandma's first concern was to see that the cafe was completely clear of people. Remaining calm, she clearly instructed all her customers and workers on how to exit the restaurant in an orderly fashion so that no one would get hurt.

It was then she realized that my brother was nowhere to be seen. She just knew that Mike, still a small child himself, may have been in the truck stop, trapped by the fire's intense heat.

With everyone else out of the restaurant, my grandmother bravely ran back in, looking for Michael, rummaging through all the stuff in the midst of the blaze. He was nowhere to be found. When Grandma could no longer bear the heat, she ran back out the front door. She cooled down for a moment, took another deep breath, and ran back in; the life of her grandson was her only concern.

She made several more trips into that inferno before someone realized what she was doing and told her that Michael had been rescued earlier by one of the customers. All this time, Michael had been sitting in Marie's car, where he was safe and secure in the comfort of the backseat.

It didn't take too long to rebuild Marie's Truck Stop Cafe, but the memory of the fire would stay with us for a long time. For the rest of her life, Grandma would have the scars of that fire up and down both her arms. But to us, those scars weren't sad or ugly. They weren't distortions of her skin, but more like badges of bravery bestowed upon a wonderful woman who thought more about others than herself.

There is another story of my grandmother's bravery that is a bit more comical. Willcox, like most small towns back then, had a curfew at night to keep kids off the streets. One evening a young boy innocently violated the curfew, but broke it nonetheless. A local police officer saw the boy and chased him down the street and into Marie's Truck Stop Cafe. The policeman was a bit overzealous, so he really started in on this poor youngster, pushing him around and generally abusing the scared kid. In today's world, if a video camera had captured what this cop was doing to this boy, it would have been another embarrassing moment for law-enforcement agencies. Well, a video camera didn't catch what was going on, but my grandmother did. From her position behind the windows that separated the eating area from the kitchen, she observed all she cared to before deciding action was necessary.

In a flash, Grandma wiped her hands on her apron, grabbed a cooking utensil, bolted out of the kitchen, pushed through the swinging door, and headed straight for the policeman. Just like a scene from an old movie, my grandmother started pounding the policeman with a rolling pin! He took some pretty direct hits, eventually running out of the restaurant for his own safety. Grandma saw to it that the young boy was taken home, and that was the end of that—except the overzealous police officer couldn't show his face in Willcox for quite some time!

Grandma's compassion knew no limitations when it came to helping other people. She loved people of all ages and cultures, and Willcox gave her the opportunity to demonstrate that love.

Because Willcox is located fewer than sixty miles from the Mexican border, we had plenty of crosscultural exposure. It was quite common to meet men, women, and children who had crossed the border in order to find a better life here in the states.

Grandma knew no such thing as prejudice. All she knew was that she cared about people, including the ones who had come from Mexico looking for work. Without any second thoughts, she would hire young Mexican women as waitresses and Mexican men as cooks or busboys. She knew they were good people who would work hard for her. All they really wanted was a break in this country.

I can still hear those grateful folks thanking her back in the restaurant's kitchen. "Señora Marie, gracias—thank you so much for hiring us. You are more than an employer…you really care about us!"

MY GRANDMA, MY MOM

I loved my grandmother. From the time I was a toddler, I would climb into her bed at night so that she could tell me a bedtime story. There were so many nights that she would come home from work so utterly exhausted that she would collapse into the bed with me.

But no matter how tired she was, she would make her best effort to tell me a story. She knew my favorite was *The Three Billy Goats Gruff.* She would start off, "OK, Teddy, here we go…'Once upon a time there were three billy goats…'"

I'd lie there, my little hands placed behind my head on her pillow, and I could just see the wicked troll she was describing. I was completely mesmerized by her. As a youngster, I was convinced my grandmother could do *anything*. She could even tell good stories.

She told them so well that on those nights when she was so completely exhausted that she would fall asleep before the story was over, I knew them well enough that *I* would tell *her* the remainder of the story, just as she had told them to me so many times earlier.

Grandma in many ways deep and profound was like my mother. My real mother was in a desperate search to find herself, so I was left in the care of a strong yet compassionate woman who genuinely did whatever she could to make my upside-down life a little more right-side-up. I still thank God that such a wonderful person raised me in my preschool years.

I am truly grateful for my Grandma's influence in my life, both in my formative years, and throughout my entire life. She taught me much, and some of her greatest lessons were still ahead for me. Always a woman of deep convictions, her spiritual journey was just beginning.

3
A TALE OF TWO FATHERS

I don't have very many memories of Ted Wills, my natural father. With my parents divorcing so early in my life, my little world centered around my grandparents, my older brother, and all the nice folks at Marie's Truck Stop Cafe. But I do remember a person who paid a visit to our town when I was four years old.

The visitor was a man from Los Angeles. He came to my grandmother's house, saying he was looking for me. He said he was a singer. "Where do you sing?" I asked with the typical curiosity of a child.

"Well, right now, I'm singing on television," he replied matter-of-factly, with a wink of his eye.

"Really?" I exclaimed.

"That's right."

"What show are you on?" I prodded.

"Right now, I am under contract to sing on *The Tennessee Ernie Ford Show*," he answered.

"Wow!" I said, my voice getting louder with each reply.

"Would you like to come to Los Angeles for a visit?" he asked me kindly. "I'd be glad to take you to the television studio."

"I…I…I don't know…" I fumbled around, looking for some sort of direction from my grandmother.

"If we use our time wisely, I imagine we can even sneak in a trip to Disneyland," he added.

"Disneyland?" I screamed.

"You bet!"

Now I was looking at Grandma with my most pleading expression.

"I don't think there would be any problem with the two of you spending some time together," Grandma spoke softly.

And so, in a flash, I was packed and driving west toward California with this man named Ted Wills—my father.

It was a wonderful visit.

We went each morning to the studio, where I watched in amazement as my dad stood up on the stage, rehearsing his part as a backup singer for Tennessee Ernie Ford. Dad took me up to the stage to meet Mr. Ford, who was as winsome in person as he always appeared in his performances. "Bring him out to the house this weekend, Ted!" Mr. Ford invited, pointing to me and grinning from ear to ear. "My wife will just love this kid!"

Before the weekend, we had other destinations to visit. As he promised, Dad took me to Disneyland, which was beyond my wildest dreams. I loved the combination of fun, action, and imagination. (Maybe that's why I like the world of professional wrestling too!)

"Are you having a good time, young man?" my father would ask, the answer obvious.

"Yes sir," I'd reply politely.

"Well, you know Walt Disney has a new feature film out in the theaters. Tomorrow, how about if we go to the movies to see *Sleeping Beauty*? Would you like that?"

"Oh, that sounds terrific!" I nodded in excited approval.

Dad took me to see the movie, and I loved it. He must have seen how I reacted to the bravery of the prince, because after the show, we hopped into his car and drove until we pulled up in front of a toy store. He walked me into that store, directed me to the display of products from *Sleeping Beauty*, and bought me a little plastic sword and shield, just like the prince's. On top of that, he added a *Sleeping Beauty* children's storybook to read later.

I was so happy.

The next day was Sunday. We slept in, then drove up into the hills outside of Hollywood to the home of Tennessee Ernie Ford. As Mr. Ford had predicted, his wife and I really hit it off. I can still remember crawling up onto her lap as she read me my brand-new *Sleeping Beauty* storybook.

THE END OF A STORY

My time with my father was very special for me. Even at the tender age of four, all I wanted to do was somehow create a bond with him. I needed a guy like Ted Wills in my life.

But our special vacation ended abruptly.

My mother had returned to Willcox after an extended road trip. When my grandmother explained where I was and with whom, Mom hit the roof. She turned on her heel, drove straight to the airport, and caught the next flight to Los

Angeles. She didn't spend much time in L.A., either. She found me, packed up my things, and we were on the airplane returning to Arizona in a blink of an eye.

My dad meant nothing bad by taking me on this trip, but my mother was quite bothered by it. Apparently, it not only upset her, but it also ate up her entire time off work. We landed in Arizona, then my mother deposited me at Grandma's house and returned to the road.

But I never forgot how wonderful that visit was with Dad. I had never really missed him before, because he had never been around long enough for me to get to know him.

I can recall thinking as a little boy, *Could I really have a dad, like my friends do?* I didn't know the answer to that question. In some ways, it was just like my trip to California. It was Fantasyland.

Mom's Change of Vocation

My mother was still on the road, but somewhere during those years, she made a job transition. She no longer traveled as a showgirl. Her job description was still physically demanding, and it was still entertaining, but she wasn't singing anymore. My mother had become a lady wrestler.

Back then, wrestling for women was a more glamorous profession than it is today. Beauty was just as important as strength, and my mother possessed them both in large quantities.

It was a transitional time for me as well, as I finally started kindergarten. I can still recall the first time my mother took me to one of her wrestling matches. At five years old, I was completely caught up in the euphoria that surrounds a live event. Mom sat me down in a section of seats that was close enough for me to see what was going on, but far enough away from the ring to keep me out of trouble.

She gave me explicit instructions: "Now you sit right here, Teddy, and don't you get up for any reason. Do you understand?"

"Yes ma'am."

"Mommy will be wrestling up there in the ring shortly, and I want you to just sit back and enjoy it, OK?"

"Yes ma'am."

She looked me deep in my eyes as she continued our conversation. "Teddy, no matter what you see happening to me up there in the ring, it is very important that you stay in your chair. Do you hear what I am saying?"

"Yes, Mom. I'll behave. Don't worry about me."

She smiled and left to change for the match. I was enthralled by the whole aura inside that arena. I don't know if this is where I first got bit by the wrestling bug, but I know I found the entire experience very stimulating.

It was *so* stimulating, in fact, that by the time my mother's match came up, I was yelling and cheering and screaming at the top of my lungs. I watched with pride as she seemed to handle her opponent with ease. But then it happened.

The match took a turn. Mom was no longer winning. Her opponent was starting to win, first gradually, then in a big way. This other woman was putting a beating on my mother! In the back of my mind I recalled my mother's warning to stay in my seat, but when she said it, certainly she didn't know that she would be getting beaten up!

I bolted out of my chair in a mixture of anger and adrenaline. "You can't do that to my mom!" I screamed as I made my way down to ringside. I was going to do all I could to help her.

But right about the time I arrived at the front row, I became paralyzed with fear. I stopped dead in my tracks. What happened next has happened to every one of us at one time or another in our lives. And we all respond the same way.

My mother glanced up from the mat and looked me straight in the eye!

The expression comes to mind, *If looks could kill*—Her stare pierced right through me. I knew I was in trouble, and I knew there was only one thing to do. I quietly turned around and went back to my seat. I believe my mother lost that match. It must have upset her, because she gave me quite a lecture all the way home.

It was awhile before I was allowed to accompany my mother to a wrestling match again.

IRON MIKE

I liked Mike DiBiase from the first time I met him.

After all, I was five years old and he took me out for an ice cream cone. How could he lose? My mother had taken me to Omaha, Nebraska, where Mike happened to be wrestling. We attended the match (I stayed in my seat), and afterwards he took me backstage to meet all the other wrestlers, who were his best buddies. Like a kid in a candy store, I was hypnotized by the whole world of professional wrestling.

I was especially awed by this man they called Iron Mike.

Mike DiBiase was the son of Italian immigrants. His father, John DiBiase, married and had three sons and a daughter before his first wife died. In the old Italian custom, John sent word back to Italy concerning his tragedy, and his second wife, Christina, was sent to him. It was through this arranged second marriage that John had two more daughters and one more son. This last son was born on December 24, 1923, in Omaha, Nebraska. They named him Michael.

In a tough part of south Omaha, Mike grew up during those difficult years of the Great Depression. His dad died while he was quite young, so Mike's uncle moved in with the family to provide a "fatherly role model" for the children.

Mike's mother was very strict. She was a mom of the old school. For example, there was a razor strap hanging in a prominent location in their small house as a reminder of what was to be endured if one disobeyed. As a more graphic example, she thought nothing of taking the steel brush that was used to scrub pots and using it to scour out the dirt that was buried deep in the creases of Mike's elbows. Think about how dirty a kid can get his elbows! Think about how painful a steel brush could be! No wonder Mike was so tough.

The DiBiases were deeply dedicated to the Roman Catholic Church. They regularly attended Saint Ann's Catholic Church in south Omaha. Mike became an altar boy at the church at an early age. He was a good student, as well as an outgoing, friendly kid. Everyone liked Mike.

Like most kids growing up in those years, Mike had a job even when he was young. In a feat that still amazes me, Mike would get up in the wee hours of the morning and board a train traveling from Omaha to Lincoln, selling newspapers to its passengers. Then, of course, he would continue his selling on the return trip. And he did all of this before he went to school each morning!

As a teenager, Mike attended Omaha Tech High School. He became a champion athlete, starring in football, track, and wrestling. In 1942, he was Tech's "King of Sports" and was named Omaha's Outstanding High School Athlete. His football abilities earned him all-city and all-state honors. In wrestling, where he competed in the heavyweight division, he won the Nebraska state wrestling championship *twice.*

By the time he graduated from high school, World War II was in full swing, so Mike fulfilled his patriotic duty by joining the navy. He was the youngest chief petty officer to serve his country. For part of his service, he was stationed in Norman, Oklahoma, where he won the Oklahoma AAU heavyweight wrestling title two years in a row. Then, he was transferred to northern California, where he won the Far Western heavyweight title; and he ultimately won the AAU national heavyweight wrestling title in New York City in April of 1946.

He ended his stint in the navy by becoming a self-defense instructor. Although still somewhat short at five feet nine inches tall, he weighed 230 pounds and had a twenty-two-inch neck. His thighs were as big as my mother's waist! He was as solid as a rock. Soon the war ended, and it was time to move on.

Mike saw a dream of his become reality when he entered the University of Nebraska after his discharge. He lettered four times in wrestling and three times in football, achieving an honor few have ever duplicated. But it wasn't without its trials.

Mike's biggest crisis came during his sophomore year. During the football season he dislocated his knee, putting him out of action for the remainder of the season. For most guys back then, an injury of that nature would have signaled the end of their careers.

But not Mike.

The following summer he put himself through a most demanding regimen of rehabilitation. He began by working eight hours a day on a job that involved intense physical labor. Once he was off work, he would travel over to Memorial Stadium at the university, where he would start at field level and run up the steps to the top of the stadium. He'd come back down and run 'em again. He did this for as long as he could. If you've ever been to that stadium, you know the steps are significantly steeper and higher than at most other stadiums.

Because of his incredible dedication to return to health, he was reinstated on the team the following season. It was because of this comeback that he was given the nickname "Iron Mike." And, of course, it stuck.

In the autumn of 1948, the entire university was abuzz with Mike's return. Omaha's local paper wrote a nice story:

> When Mike DiBiase trots onto the field for the Huskers, he'll deserve the loudest kind of cheer. He's a courageous young man who has overcome terrific odds to land a place on the Husker line.... Those running trips up and down the aisles of the stadium did more than cut off his

excess poundage. They put his injured leg to a strenuous test—and made it stronger than ever before. Mike's knee has given him no trouble at all in the first three weeks of practice. He shows a lot of drive in the line; a willingness to mix it up where the real action takes place in football.

Here's hoping the solid little guy has a big year. He deserves it.

Mike excelled in every area of life. He even became a local favorite in Omaha for his heroic deeds off the athletic field. It seemed only natural that one summer morning Omaha awakened to see this headline in the newspaper:

Mike DiBiase Flags Train As Locked Car Blocks Tracks

Below the bold print, the following story appeared:

Stocky Mike DiBiase, University of Nebraska football tackle working this summer on the police department, pitted his great hulk, his hopes and a madly waving flashlight against a Rock Island train early Monday morning and emerged a victor. The train, with its own powerful beam glaring in Mike's eyes, came to a halt only three inches from an automobile locked on the tracks at 25th and Randolph.

The vehicle was sitting at a slant, the police report said, with the right rear wheel and fender resting on the tracks, making it impossible to push it off either manually or with another vehicle.

DiBiase ran north on the tracks to meet the southbound Rock Island Number 7, while patrolman Clarence Miller went to 19th and O to try to intercept the train at the station.

Miller's attempts at using a spotlight and siren to halt the train were unsuccessful, but the engineer heeded DiBiase's flashlight.

It reads almost like a fairy tale. Iron Mike stars in football, stars in wrestling, and even stops speeding trains three inches from disaster!

Mike certainly got into his share of mischief, but overall he was a fine example of a young man. The whole town knew big things were ahead for this likable fellow; they just didn't know what path he would take.

By the time he was ready to graduate in June of 1950, Mike was being courted by several of the best teams in professional football, including the

Chicago Bears, who were hot after his services on the offensive and defensive lines.

But Iron Mike was drawn to a different kind of athletic pursuit. Right out of college, he began his career in professional wrestling. Initially, he decided to wrestle only until the football tryouts, but he fell in love with the sport.

Wrestling's gain was football's loss.

A NEW DAD

From the first time Iron Mike entered my life, he was an influence for good. Sure, he had his share of weaknesses, but he was a man I could respect, even with his shortcomings. He affected me in ways I am still coming to realize.

While researching our family archives for the writing of this book, I came across an article that had been written about Mike in 1969. The source was the local newspaper in his hometown of Omaha, Nebraska. A two-page spread featured my hero in the Sunday magazine. I couldn't take my eyes off the page as I read the reporter's words about the man he called "The Bad Guy:"

> Here was an anomaly, for sure. I sat down to chat with Iron Mike DiBiase about what it's like to make a living as a veteran "bad guy" professional rassler, but somehow the talk veered.
>
> Iron Mike was saying that today's moral tone worries him; that parents who let their kids run wild without knowing who their companions are have got rocks in their heads.
>
> He was commenting that young people who grow up without respect for their parents may have no respect for anything, including God.
>
> He has been known to give his own kids mouth-soapings for telling lies, even little ones—spare the rod, spoil the child, etc.
>
> The talk went along this line for some time—and perhaps it wasn't so anomalous, after all. A professional rassler is in a good position to observe the general scene and Iron Mike does have five sons and two daughters.
>
> Still the philosophy seemed strange coming from him...

I stared at those words for a long time. There was something profound about how this writer described Mike DiBiase. Through his words, I learned a little bit more about how Iron Mike had influenced me.

For with a few minor changes, it could have been an article about me.

At five years old, I was ecstatic when Iron Mike DiBiase came into my life. And my time with him was to become much more than an occasional visit to a wrestling match.

Not long after their first meeting, Iron Mike married my mother.

4
AVOIDING OVEREXPOSURE

When Iron Mike DiBiase married my mother, I got more than a new dad. I also got a new name.

Mike legally adopted me shortly after his new marriage, so from 1959 on, I was known as Ted DiBiase. How did it feel to change names? With the incredible love and respect I had already developed for Iron Mike, it felt *great*.

Technically, Iron Mike should be considered my stepfather. But in reality, he was the only father I ever knew. When people would refer to him as my stepdad, it would irritate me, as it continues to do to this day. He was Dad.

Mike became the father I had never had. Granted, he wasn't flawless. His marriage to my mother was his second. He and his first wife had four children. But after their divorce, she and their children left Omaha and moved back to her hometown of Napa, in the wine country of northern California. I'm sure there was tension in that set of circumstances, but Mike had moved on, willingly taking up life with my mother and her two sons.

A New Home

We finished out the school year in Willcox, but after kindergarten it was time to move on. With mixed feelings, I said good-bye to Grandma, and we headed east to our new home of Amarillo, Texas. It was quite a transition for a six-year-old boy, leaving the warmth and security of the only home I had known to take up residence with this woman who used to visit and her new husband. But, there again, I was so mesmerized by the heroics of Iron Mike DiBiase that I would have followed them anywhere.

Homesickness happened, however. One day after we had settled in Amarillo, I started whining about wanting to go back to Willcox to live with Grandma. Most likely, either my mom or dad had said or done something to make me angry, so, like any child, I used Willcox as a ploy to get them to lighten up on me.

"Now you just hush, Teddy," my mom said, trying to avoid a nasty scene over nothing.

"No!" I persisted defiantly. "I wanna go back to live with my grandma! I don't like it here!"

Usually my parents would blow it off, but on this particular occasion, it was all Mike could stand. "OK, Teddy, if that's what you want, that's what we will do," he said to my complete surprise. "Are you 100 percent sure that's what you want?" he inquired one last time.

"Yes," I answered, this time a bit softer.

"All right, Helen, let's pack him a bag and drive him down to the bus station. We'll put him on the next bus to Willcox."

Going to my grandmother's house usually sounded so pleasant, but I was feeling very uncomfortable about this spontaneous excursion. Acting on my request, my parents were putting some clothes and toys in a little suitcase, getting me ready to move back with Grandma.

We all piled into our car to begin the drive to the bus station. Along the way downtown, we passed the movie theater. We craned our necks to see what was advertised on the marquee. Mike bellowed, "Look, Butch!" (Butch was the new nickname for my older brother.) "*Peter Pan* is playing here!"

"Yeah, that's great!" he answered.

"Isn't that the movie we've been wanting to see for a while now?" Mike pondered out loud.

"That's right," my mom chimed in. "We've just been waiting for it to come to town."

"Well, I've got an idea," Mike continued, the three of them acting as if I weren't even in the car. "How does it sound to everyone if we drop Teddy off at the bus station and then we'll all go see *Peter Pan*?"

Mom and my brother cheered and applauded Mike's great idea, while I sat in the backseat in a real quandary. *If I go to Grandma's, I'll miss the movie,* I thought to myself. *And why do I really want to leave, anyway? It's not so bad here with Mom and Dad.*

The more I thought about it, the more I decided to make a course correction on our journey.

We never made it to the bus depot…

We all loved *Peter Pan.*

I didn't lose touch with my grandmother, even though I moved away. I received letters from her all the time, thanks to Mike's diligence in keeping her informed about all my childhood activities.

There was more to this guy than just a big, strong wrestler. That he would so consistently correspond with Grandma says a lot about what made him tick.

MY DAD, MY HERO

Mike was my hero, and just watching him live his life inspired me. I can still recall playing with a couple of girls from our neighborhood one warm Amarillo afternoon. We were playing catch with a rubber ball. One of us missed the throw, and the ball went bouncing beyond our yard, right over a fence that enclosed a pretty ferocious-sounding dog.

"I'll go get it!" one of the girls yelled before any of us could even think about the possible danger of the situation. She scaled the fence, jumped into the next yard, and headed straight for the ball, while a little boy and girl watched wide-eyed from the safety of the other side of the fence.

The dog immediately saw the intruder and began to bark more fiercely than we had ever heard. The poor little girl took one look at the dog and panicked. Dogs can smell fear, and he knew he had this youngster right where he wanted her. He attacked while she stood frozen.

As I watched this scary scene, I thought about what Iron Mike would do if he were here. That's all I needed to think about, and I was over the fence in a flash. I ran up behind that dog and grabbed him by his back two legs. With all the strength I could muster, I yanked him away from my friend, lifting him high over my head, and tossed him behind my back! Now it was the poor dog's turn to be frightened, and he ran away whimpering!

I helped my playmate back to our yard. She was quite upset, because the dog had taken a pretty big piece of skin out of her right inner arm. By then, parents had come upon the scene to take good care of us all.

That incident became a real highlight of my first-grade year in Amarillo. I had achieved a bit of hero status and received praise from people all over town. It felt really good, but the best praise of all came from my own home. Iron Mike was very proud of his son. What a great feeling for a kid of six!

MOVING ON—AGAIN

In those days, wrestling was very much a regional sport. A guy would come into an area and wrestle there as long as he could before becoming "overexposed." When that happened, it was time to move on.

For Mike, it happened in less than a year in Amarillo. Before I had ev finished the first grade, we had relocated to a new region where Mike could do his thing all over again.

We moved to Portland, Oregon.

The move took place right around the Christmas holidays. I finished up the year of 1960 in Amarillo, then we traveled to Willcox to spend Christmas with my grandmother. We had a new family member with us by this time. My younger brother John was born in November of that year, right before we left Amarillo. As I recall, Mom was off having her baby while I was trying to make sense of the Nixon-Kennedy debates, which were being televised.

After a pleasant visit with my mom's family, it was off to Portland. Butch decided that he wanted to stay in Willcox with Grandma, so Mom, Dad, baby John, and I made the trip north. Even though we moved so much (and I have plenty of moves still ahead in my story), these were wonderful years for me. I had a family. I had a mom and a dad. It meant so much that we were all together, even with the crazy schedules of travel that wrestling demanded. I was very happy.

My most vivid memory of Portland is that it rained all the time. (Bet you never heard that before, have you?) But I do recall one incident that I'd probably rather forget. It was a time I got in trouble with my dad.

THE DIRT-CLOD INCIDENT

I was down the street playing in a yard that was in the process of being redone. Thus, there were these little dirt clods all over the ground. Little boys love to throw dirt clods, especially against a wall. They look like little bombs exploding, and that's cool stuff for a little kid!

I was usually pretty good about my aim too. But in the middle of all my perfect throws, one got away from me. And, of course, instead of hitting a wall, it hit a little girl I was playing with. It was bad, too, because it didn't hit her on the knee or the arm, but square on the face. She stood there screaming, blood running down from a cut on the side of her nose. Her mom, hearing the commotion, sprinted out to the scene of the crime. I was caught, so I didn't run.

"I'm really sorry, ma'am," I apologized. "It was an accident, honest! I didn't mean to hit her. I was throwing them over toward that wall over there," I pointed as I pleaded my case.

Once she determined her daughter was all right, she said to me. "OK, young man, my daughter is going to be just fine." I smiled with a relieved sigh.

"However," she continued, "I think you should go back home and tell your parents what happened, and that will be the end of it."

I nodded, told her I would tell my folks right away, and ran like the dickens before she came up with any other ideas. Retelling this scene to my parents might sound innocent enough, but in my world, I knew I was going to get it if I confessed this to my folks. Mom and Dad had both warned me countless times about throwing rocks. I wasn't sure they would see the difference between a rock and a dirt clod, so I decided not to chance it.

I walked up to the front door of our house and froze. I just couldn't bring myself to tell them what had happened. I turned on my heel and ran away, heading somewhere I would feel safe with my secret.

Perhaps I could have bluffed my way through all of this mess had it not been for the little girl's mother, who made a surprise visit to our home later that same day.

"Is Teddy here?" the lady asked my mom.

"No, he's not back from playing yet," Mom replied. "Why are you looking for him?"

"Because I sent him home to tell you what happened. He promised me he would do it."

With that, my parents became aware of the whole "Dirt-Clod Incident." Mike was furious.

I finally returned home later that day, resolved to keep my secret a secret. "I just came by to check in," I said, trying to act as normal as possible. "I'm gonna go down to play in the park," I added.

"Teddy, before you go…is there anything you want to tell us?"

"No."

That's all it took. Mike lowered the boom. "Well, sit right down here, young man," he began, working hard to keep his cool. "We know all about what happened down the street today."

I sat down and swallowed hard.

"You know how we feel about you throwing rocks," Mike began. "But what bothers me the most is that *you lied.* You told that little girl's mother that you would come right home and tell us what happened. You didn't. We even asked you if you wanted to tell us anything and you said, 'No.' You lied to her and you lied to us, Teddy. We're not raising you to become a liar."

I remember how bad I felt in disappointing Mike. I just wanted him to take me over his knee and give me a few swats with his belt. But his discipline was to be even more agonizing.

"You need to be punished for your disobedience," Dad spoke calmly.

"Yes, sir, I know," I replied.

"I've narrowed it down to two options," he went on. "The first option is to be grounded from playing with any of your friends for a whole week. The second option is for your mother and me to add extra chores to your schedule."

All I could do was look at the ground. I knew that between the two options, being grounded was definitely more severe for me. I didn't know which he would pick.

"You need to learn responsibility," he continued. "So I think I'll have you decide your own punishment."

I looked up at him in shock.

"So, which one will it be?"

I felt like I deserved the harder of the two, so I chose option one. He nodded, knowing I had chosen the more difficult one. He appreciated my sacrifice.

Knowing how hard it was on me, three days into the grounding, Mike took me aside to tell me how proud he was of me for taking this incident so seriously. Because he had seen that the lesson had been learned, he reduced my sentence by a couple of days. He was tough, but fair. He was a good dad.

NEXT STOP: HOUSTON

Portland was a fun experience for me, but like the other towns, it was soon time to move on. The next stop on Iron Mike's wrestling circuit was Houston, Texas. I attended second grade in Houston. My brother Mike rejoined us that year as well. The five of us were doing just fine.

School was different for me in Houston because my parents decided to enroll me in a Catholic school rather than a public school. It was a shock to my system to move from the more relaxed schedule of public school to the strict demands of parochial education. I didn't respond well. I wasn't motivated by the sisters. I just wasn't willing to apply myself, and my only excitement was play time. I really lost interest in my studies, and nothing seemed to turn me around.

Nothing, that is, until the sisters decided to sit me down to tell me that, if I didn't improve my grades, I would be held back from going on to the third grade. Suddenly, I was motivated. I came on with a strong finish and moved on to the third grade on schedule.

Before I actually completed second grade, however, we had already picked everything up and moved again! This time we headed west to some familiar territory. We moved back to Willcox.

MY OTHER HERO

The nice thing about having a year of Catholic school under my belt was that it sure made third grade a breeze back in the public school. I was a pretty typical eight-year-old, enjoying life and having a good time.

One of my loves had become watching old science-fiction movies on television. I considered the Werewolf and Frankenstein good friends of mine. My favorite night was Saturday evening, when the local station would run a double feature called *Saturday Night Chiller*.

Sometimes I would watch the show at my grandmother's house, then run home to our little place. If I happened to arrive home and no one was there, it could get kind of spooky. One particular evening after watching the movies, Mike sent me home ahead of him, promising to follow shortly. I reluctantly agreed, because deep down I didn't want to be at that house all alone. I ran from Grandma's house to the other house, unlocked the door, and sped inside, locked the door behind me, turned on every light in the place and checked for anything suspicious. One by one, I turned off the lights and eventually got into bed. In the darkness, I couldn't sleep. I just kept waiting for Mike to arrive. All I wanted to hear was the sound of the back door opening and shutting. But all I heard was silence.

Then I thought I heard the back door quietly open and close.

"Mike, is that you?" I asked the empty room.

There was no answer.

Then I thought I heard a footstep or two, followed by more silence, more fear, more resolve not to watch any more of those movies ever again.

"Come on, Mike, I know it's you," I said again, wanting to believe my own words. "Answer me!"

Stillness and silence. I was about to conclude that this incident was all part of my imagination—I thought I'd had about enough fear for one night— when, out of nowhere, a person leaped from the darkness and landed on top of me as I trembled on my bed...

It was Mike.

I was so scared that I screamed at the top of my lungs, while simultaneously wetting my pants.

It was a scary night, but the fact remains that on my list of heroes, right under Iron Mike was my older brother. He was very influential in bringing me closer to a sport I fell in love with immediately—football.

My dad had been a football star, but that was before my time. When Mike got involved in playing for his high school team, I was at an impressionable age. I'd sweet-talk my way into accompanying him to his football practices, where I would run up and down the sidelines like an up-and-coming star. I'd hit those tackling dummies as hard as I could too! And happiest of all, I can still remember the ecstasy I felt when my parents got me a football uniform, specially sized for an eight-year-old, as a Christmas gift that year. It didn't take me long to determine that I wanted to be a football player. I wanted to be one right then. I wanted to grow up and play for a high school team, then a college team, and then the pros. Mike was a great influence on me. He was the star tight end on the varsity squad. He also played on the basketball team and was an excellent student.

GETTING ON WITH GOD—IN OMAHA

Things looked good in Willcox for everyone except Dad. At thirty-nine, he was growing weary of the grinding road schedule that was demanded of a professional wrestler. But, try as he might, it still wasn't the right time to retire and settle down. With mixed feelings, our family packed its bags one more time for a move back to Mike's hometown: Omaha, Nebraska.

I had visited Omaha before, but this was the first time I was going to live there. We moved into Dad's house, the place he had lived with his first wife and kids. They were in California, so there was enough room for all of us.

Slipping into some of his old patterns, Mike started back to the church in which he had grown up. Saint Ann's Catholic Church and School was only one block from our house. Between our house and the church was Columbus Park, a great place to run and play.

We started regularly attending Saint Ann's. We had attended the Catholic Church in Willcox, and I was immediately drawn to the atmosphere of worship in the sanctuary. I wanted to know God. I can still remember how desperately I wanted to become an altar boy. I had memorized all the Latin responses to the prayers that were required for the position. I was so happy the day the priest told me that I could join in that coveted position of altar boy. I took it seriously. The move to Omaha only strengthened my commitment to my faith.

I took God seriously, even at a young age. I wanted to know Him. I credit Mike for instilling that desire in me. I saw that God was important to him, so He became important to me.

My four-year-old brother was my first "disciple." Because we shared a bedroom in our tiny Omaha home, John would learn about Bible doctrine whether or not he wanted to. Each night before crawling into bed, we would kneel together at the foot of our beds as I would teach him to memorize the Lord's Prayer and the Apostle's Creed. When he was finally old enough to go to school, he also went to the Catholic school. John came home that first day and excitedly shared with me how amazed the nuns were at all the "stuff" I had already taught him.

To many children, reciting Christian truths was an exercise in frustration—meaningless words strung together in senseless sentences. But for me, it was all very real. It was more than reciting words. I listened to them, I thought about them, and God spoke to me through them. Looking back now, I am humbled that God would choose to speak to me at such an early age.

GETTING SERIOUS ABOUT FOOTBALL

We lived in Omaha for two years. I attended fourth and fifth grade at Saint Ann's. The whole thing was a bit surreal, because I was living in the very same neighborhood where Dad had grown up. My friends were the children of his friends. And just like Mike, I got really serious about football.

Saint Ann's had a football team for its seventh and eighth graders, but I was determined, even as a fourth grader, that I was going to make the team. And I did. I wanted to follow in my father's footsteps. I can still remember sitting in bed, late at night, staring at the ceiling, thinking to myself, *If I can be as much like Dad as possible, then I will be successful.*

That was OK with Mike, with one major exception: "DON'T EVEN THINK ABOUT GOING INTO PRO WRESTLING!" he would scream. And he meant it. At this time in his life, Mike was desperately trying to get out of the wrestling business. He linked up with a friend who was running a nightclub and tried his hand at that for a while. He also tried selling insurance. Neither venture provided any long-term success, and before long, Mike was wrestling again.

I Wanna Be Like Mike

Like any kid that age, I was beginning to feel the effects of peer pressure. My mother noticed this situation and would comment to me: "Teddy, your father went through the same thing! Not only are you growing up where he grew up, but you should also try to develop the same approach to life. He wasn't one of the crowd, and you don't have to be, either. You both have plans, goals, strategies. He didn't achieve what he has achieved by giving into peer pressure. And you can be just like him."

She was right. Sure, I had friends, but I wanted to show my friends that I didn't need to smoke or drink to be popular. I could achieve popularity through better ways.

After fifth grade, we moved to Amarillo again, but only for a year.

Then, Mike decided that he could return to Omaha and use it as a base for travel to all the different regions he still needed to frequent in his world of wrestling.

I spent the next three years back in Omaha—the biggest block of time in one place that I could recall in my life. They were important years for me too. Mike saw how serious I was about football, but I was unable to play in seventh and eighth grade because Saint Ann's no longer had a football program. The next time I would play would be in ninth grade, upon entering high school.

During those years in Omaha, I asked Mike to help me train. "If you're wanting to play football because you really want to, that's fine," he would say. "But if you're doing this because you think you have to because I did—don't do it."

"I'm doing this 'cause I want to," I would respond.

"OK. Well, then, I'll help you. If you really want my help, don't forget, you asked for it," he would continue his warning. "I'll work you hard."

"I want it, sir," I answered back eagerly.

Then he would look me straight in the eye and add, "Just remember, Teddy, I love you no matter what. Be the best you can be at whatever it is you do."

It was just what I needed to hear. I would kneel each night at my bed and pray: "Dear God, please give me the athletic ability I need to succeed at my goals. More than anything, I want to be just like my dad. Amen."

I'm glad those years were a time of learning to depend on the Lord. It would be an important lesson for me. I had no idea what was about to happen in my life during the next year. I would never be the same.

5
TRAGEDY IN THE RING

Those years between kindergarten and ninth grade were filled with warm memories, lots of moves, and family closeness. Did you catch all the geography we covered? Here's a quick review:

Willcox, Arizona: Kindergarten
Amarillo, Texas: First grade (first half)
Portland, Oregon: First grade (second half)
Houston, Texas: Second grade
Willcox, Arizona: Third grade
Omaha, Nebraska: Fourth and fifth grade
Amarillo, Texas: Sixth grade
Omaha, Nebraska: Seventh, eighth, and ninth grade

On the road? You bet! But we were a family that really looked out for each other. I knew that my father and mother really loved me, and that was all I needed to be happy in my childhood.

BACK TO AMARILLO

After my freshman year in high school, once again, it was time to move on. We had made Omaha a real "home base" for our family, but the threat of overexposure continued to keep professional wrestlers and their families on the move. We packed up everything and headed south…to Amarillo, Texas.

There was an entire region of wrestling in the west Texas area that was known simply as the "Amarillo territory." Naturally, the city of Amarillo itself was the center of the action. Normally, we would have left most of our stuff back in Omaha, knowing we'd eventually return. But this move was different. We took everything. Mike was eager to reach the end of his career, and he felt that Amarillo was the perfect place to finish it out. In another year or so, he would be all ready for us to make one final move. He envisioned us moving back to Arizona.

When we arrived in Amarillo one morning in early June, we moved right into an apartment complex that was adequate for our family. There were nicer apartments around, so we kept our ears open for any vacancies. Mike was already busy back on the circuit, Mom was doing her thing, my little brother John was happy, and I was able to reacquaint myself with my old friends from sixth grade. My days were filled either with hanging out with the old gang or working out in my room with my weights that I had moved from Omaha. I was lifting every day, getting bigger and stronger, moving toward my goals revolving around football.

Toward the end of June, we were alerted that an apartment was opening up in a more desirable complex. No sooner had we emptied all the old, brown, cardboard boxes we had brought from Omaha, than we were repacking them for this small move down the road to a nicer place.

Dad's Last Move

It was Wednesday, July 2, 1969. Summer had arrived, so it was a hot, humid, west Texas day. Dad and I had a full agenda this particular morning. He and I moved all our furniture from the old apartment to the new one. It took longer than we anticipated, morning turning into afternoon. But it was a good time for me, as I look back. Working side by side with Dad gave me a little more time with him than the typical day allowed. I was so pleased that I could keep up with him in all the heavy lifting as well. All the work on those weights was paying off!

We spent the day working and enjoying the sort of idle chatter a father and his son engage in during hours of lifting and loading.

"Your mother will really like this place," he said, smiling broadly. He was always thinking of ways to make my mother's life a little more pleasant.

"Yeah, Dad, this place is a lot nicer than the one we're in right now," I answered from the other side of a couch we were carrying in. Before long, we were both huffing and puffing.

"And what about you?" he asked, once he caught his breath. "You are all set to attend a great school this fall."

"I know, sir."

"Teddy, it's a good school academically, but it's also a good school for *football!*" he exclaimed, smiling even bigger with that contagious toothy grin. "If you work hard, good things could happen."

"I hope so!" I added enthusiastically, my thoughts drifting to waves of people cheering in a stadium where I had just made an amazing play in the private world of my daydreams.

"It's gonna happen," he said softly, "as long as you work hard."

I looked over at him, noticing how happy he was. Sure, he was working hard. He was breathing heavily, sweating freely, and he looked a little flushed. But he was happy. And that made me feel good.

His happiness meant a lot to me, especially in these days when he'd come home after a match or a long trip completely exhausted. None of us had ever seen Dad so tired. Mom was worried about him, to the point that she kept pushing him to take some time off.

"Talk to Dory, Mike," she'd coax. "He'll understand. He'll give you some well-deserved vacation time."

Dad was working for Dory Funk, one of his best friends. As the promoter in the Amarillo area, Dory was a master at his job. Publicly, he and Dad were perceived as "the worst of enemies." But they had a friendship beneath it all that was genuine.

Dad had jokingly approached Dory earlier about the possibility of getting a little time off, but Dory had not taken him seriously. Dad, always grateful to be working, didn't push it any further. We all wished he would have.

After we had moved everything into the new apartment, Mom and John came over for their first look. We all loved it! Mom started in on dinner. In honor of our first night in a new place, one of Mike's favorite dinners was on the menu. Soon the warm smells of spaghetti and meatballs filled the cozy apartment.

It was a pretty typical dinner: Mom watched Dad, John, and me pile on the pasta and sauce and then eat like we hadn't eaten in a week. The conversation didn't include anything too profound, just a mixture of excitement to be in a nicer place along with the laziness of a warm summer evening.

"I'll clean up the kitchen for you guys," I volunteered, once again noticing how tired Dad looked.

"That's real nice of you, Teddy," Mom replied. "Mike, why don't the two of us go take a little nap for a few minutes before you have to go to your match. I think you'll feel better if you do."

Mike didn't argue, following Mom into their new bedroom. As I stacked dishes in the sink, I couldn't believe that after a whole day of heavy moving, Mike still had to drive down to a match in Lubbock, a hundred miles south of Amarillo. What endurance this guy had!

Mom and Dad had been in their bedroom less than five minutes when a knock on our door interrupted our quiet evening. It was the apartment manager from down the hall. "Tell your dad he has a phone call down at my place," the man informed me. Because we had just moved in that day, our phone hadn't been connected yet. As much as I hated doing so, I tapped on the bedroom door, and Mike was on his feet and down the hall in a flash.

Just a few minutes later he returned. "That was Art Nelson," he informed us. Art was another local wrestler. "He's gonna give me a ride down to Lubbock, but we need to leave early for a meeting, so he's on his way over."

So much for Dad's nap.

Dad threw his gear into his bag, splashed some water on his face, kissed my mom good-bye, waved to John and me, and bolted out the door. This was his life, and we were all used to it. He had hustled out our front door a thousand times before in the same manner.

We had no idea that when he sprinted out that door it would be the last time any of us would ever see him alive.

RECEIVING THE NEWS

Our evening went on as usual. I linked up with some of my friends and headed over to a local park to see some of my buddies playing baseball. We laughed, cheered, and goofed off like typical fifteen-year-olds. When we returned, I walked up to the hall in front of our apartment, plopped down on the carpet, and started talking with two sisters who lived in the same building. I had known Jaynet Foreman and her sister Dana from living in Amarillo three years ago. We were having a good time reminiscing about the old days. (Jaynet would play a big part in my life later on.)

The main door downstairs opened slowly. From my vantage point upstairs, I could see Barbara Kane. Her husband, Jack, was a wrestling manager here in town. Barbara was accompanied by Dorothy Funk, Dory's ex-wife. We had known both of these couples as friends for years, so I never gave it a second thought when they showed up at our place.

"Teddy, where is your mother?" Barbara asked, a more serious tone in her voice than I recalled hearing before.

"She's in the apartment sleeping, ma'am," I answered.

"You need to wake her up right away. We need to talk with her. It's very important."

"What's up?" I asked, sensing something was wrong.

"Just go wake your mother up, Teddy."

I raced into the apartment, walked back to my mom's room, and started shaking her in her bed. My mom is one sound sleeper, and I was not having any success in waking her.

"Don't worry, Teddy," Barbara said softly behind me. "We have to take your mother to Lubbock."

"Please tell me what this is all about," I persisted.

"Teddy, I'm afraid your dad's had a heart attack, and they've rushed him to the hospital."

I stood in stunned silence when our apartment manager raced into our place announcing that there was an emergency phone call for a woman named Barbara. They ran down the hall together, leaving me in my own state of shock.

Before I had much time to think through what this was all about, Barbara returned with the horrible news.

"Barbara, don't lie to me," I began. "What's going on?"

She took a deep breath, her eyes already filled with tears, and said, "Teddy, your Dad just died."

Immediately I started to cry. I left the bedroom, walking around in tearful, dazed disbelief. The severity of the situation weighed heavier on me with each step. *This can't be happening! What will I do without Dad in my life? How can I possibly go on without him?* The questions ran through my head in streams of sadness and grief. Then it hit me....

"Oh my God! My mom!" I blurted out, running back to her side. We finally got her awake. With Barbara on one side of her and Dorothy on the other, they broke the tragic news. "Helen, Mike's dead."

Mom became hysterical. She was immediately out of control. "No, no, no!" she screamed at the top of her lungs. "This can't be true!"

We weren't able to control her. Fortunately, Barbara's husband, Jack, showed up at that moment, and he helped us restrain her. He actually had to slap her, yelling, "Helen, you've got to get a grip!"

Barbara's daughter had taken my little brother to get a cold drink while we were dealing with all this bad news. When he returned home, he could see by everyone's expressions that something was wrong. I don't know how it ended up happening this way, but I was the one who told my little brother the news of Dad's death.

I took John into his bedroom. The poor kid looked pretty shaken up, and he didn't know what was going on yet. I didn't know what I was going to say to make it any easier on this little guy. I remembered what Dad had said when his mother died: "She's at peace now," he whispered. "She's looking down on us now." Those thoughts helped me a little bit.

I swallowed hard, looked deep into John's concerned eyes, and spoke. "Dad died tonight, John."

Before I could say another word, my little brother threw his arms around me and began to sob uncontrollably. Before long we were both crying, holding on to each other as tightly as we could. In one of God's little miracles, John suddenly pulled away from me to tell me what he was thinking:

"Teddy, Dad's at peace. He's looking down on us right now. He's fine."

We spent the night at Barbara's house that evening. No one slept though. I remember just tossing and turning, crying softly the entire night. Two questions kept overwhelming my mind:

Why?

And *why now?*

DEALING WITH THE LOSS

The next morning we stayed at Jack and Barbara's house. While we were there, some wrestlers who had been with Dad when he died came over to visit, share their condolences, and explain some of the missing details.

I tried hard to hold it together, but it wasn't easy. Iron Mike meant everything to me. Among the guys who came over was Terry Funk, who brought with him an unexpected item: Dad's wrestling bag. I asked for it, unzipped it, and pulled out its contents. As I rummaged through his stuff, lifting item after item out of the bag, it was too much for me. There were his wrestling tights, his socks, his shoes, all still wet with his perspiration. It all still smelled like him.

I buried my face in his clothes, clinging to the last part of my dad I could, weeping like a baby. As the guys tried to console me, one more item dropped out of Dad's bag. It was a set of rosary beads. My dad loved God. Now he was with Him. They were together in a better place.

After I regained my composure, one of the wrestlers, Harley Race, sat us down to tell us exactly what had happened in Lubbock that tragic Wednesday night of July 2, 1969.

Iron Mike was wrestling a huge guy known as Man Mountain Mike. The match was going along as scheduled when Man Mountain Mike picked up Dad and threw him out of the ring. Dad crawled back in but was immediately pushed out again, this time on the other side of the ring.

Dad got back up and wearily reached for the second rope of the ring in order to get back in. He held the rope for an extra moment, then collapsed, and fell face down on the floor.

Back then, the rules allowed you a count of twenty to get back in the ring. The referee began slowly calling off the numbers, but all the while he knew that this was not going according to plan.

"I could see he wasn't moving at all," Harley told us that morning after. "I was standing in the back, but I knew something was wrong. This wasn't the way it was supposed to be."

He raced down to ringside, knelt next to Dad, and rolled him over on his back. "I knew right away he'd had a heart attack," Harley said softly. "I pounded on his chest, I gave him mouth-to-mouth, I did everything I could. I will say this: When I felt his wrist, he did have a pulse. It was very weak, but he was still alive."

"Come on, Mike, hang in there!" Harley had exhorted him.

But Dad didn't respond.

By then, the ambulance had arrived to take him to a local hospital. He was pronounced dead on the emergency room table.

An autopsy was performed, and it revealed that Dad had arterial sclerosis (hardening of the arteries), with one artery to his heart completely blocked. They also found scar tissue around his heart, indicating he'd had previous heart attacks. If he knew about his heart condition, Mike certainly never said anything to us.

Years later, I found out he had visited our doctor when we were still living in Omaha. It was our family physician, Dr. McNamara, who had cautioned him to stop wrestling. But Dad was stubborn. He didn't listen. He didn't even slow down.

It was all coming together now. There had been some warning signs, even in the last week of his life. Seven days before he died, he was wrestling locally in Amarillo. After the match I remember seeing him in a way I had never seen him before. The only way to describe it was "disoriented." For a guy who was in familiar surroundings, he had no idea where he was. We thought it was odd but didn't give it much thought beyond that moment.

Three days later, he was running an errand. It was Sunday afternoon, and he threw us boys into the car to pick up a couple of items down the street at the local convenience store. It was all very uneventful, except when he parked the car. Out in clear view for all of us to see was a large pole. Driving as if he never noticed it, Mike sideswiped that pole. How he could have missed seeing it was beyond me, but again, I didn't give it much thought at the time.

And then there was the actual day he died. Mike had spent the day lifting heavy furniture. He was exhausted, and he tried to sneak in a little nap but never got the chance. He ate a heavy meal, probably too close to match time. Add to it a lifetime of smoking and eating rich foods, and it's a little easier to understand why Iron Mike's body finally gave out on him.

Saying Good-bye

Saturday, July 5, 1969, we had a funeral service for Mike at a local funeral home. I had only been to one funeral before, the one for Mike's mom. The shock of seeing my hero in the casket was jolting. He looked so handsome in his blue suit. I thought at any moment he would sit up to greet me.

When it was time to close the casket, I lost it one last time. I didn't want them to close the lid. Hysterical, I had to be pulled away from the casket so the service could continue. I was at such a loss.

We had his body shipped to Arizona. Mom, John, and I quietly got in our car and drove to Willcox, where Dad was buried. We knew that there was no way we were going to stay in Amarillo. We drove back, packed our things, and retraced our route. We were once again moving to Willcox.

Lasting Lessons from Mike

It was so hard for me to let go. Everything reminded me of Iron Mike. His death was eighteen days before the United States's first moon landing. We were listening to songs on the radio like "Sugar, Sugar" by the Archies, as well as tunes from Three Dog Night and the Grass Roots. To this day, when songs are played from that time, I am immediately transported back to that feeling of sadness.

Yet, in the midst of all that grief, I never felt bitterness. I never yelled at God. I asked why plenty of times, but I never argued. I wasn't bitter, but I didn't understand it either.

But God will always take something bad and make something good out of it. When I settled in Willcox for my tenth-grade year, I discovered I had a determination that was stronger than ever. "I won't give up!" I would mumble under my breath, to nobody in particular. "I won't quit, because of all Dad has instilled in me." And I meant it.

The obvious place for that determination to demonstrate itself was on the football field. In my first triumph during our preseason practices, I made the varsity football team as a tenth grader. Then, I was named a starter on the varsity— going both ways. By the time the first game arrived, I was the starting offensive tackle and defensive tackle, ready for the best season of my life.

There was a very vivid memory in place in my mind right before I took the field for the first varsity game of my career. As the marching band proudly played the opening strains of our national anthem, I blocked everything else out of my mind for a moment of silence. In that quiet moment, I made a very important dedication: *This game is for you, Dad,* I whispered. *I know you are not here physically. But I know you are watching me. This is for you.*

And then, I prayed to the Lord: *Dear Lord, please give me this one. This is for my dad. This is the beginning of my goal. Thank You, Lord. Amen.*

By the time I finished my prayer, there were huge tears streaming down my cheeks. I wiped my face on my jersey, strapped on my helmet, and ran on to the playing field with a new resolve.

That night, a wonderful thing happened. God heard my sincere words and chose to answer my prayer. I had a most productive game. By the time the final gun sounded, I had made twelve unassisted tackles, blocked a punt, knocked down a pass, and recovered a fumble.

It was the greatest game I had ever played.

6
ACHIEVING A GOAL
NEVER BEFORE ACHIEVED

The determination to excel athletically because of Mike's death, combined with the time he had spent with me in training the summer before, meant that I was destined to have a great season in football.

To this day, I still believe that a person can be or do whatever he or she desires if that person will only take it to the Lord first. When you pray, read the Scriptures, and seek God's direction, He will let you know if it's the way He wants you to go. When His direction is clear, then the rest of the equation is simply stated: *Work!*

THANKS, DAD!

Just a year before, I had spent the summer with Dad in a very intense workout program that was specifically designed to get me in the best possible shape to play football. I remember recruiting a buddy of mine named Oscar to work out with me. Initially, he was excited to join in, but it got tough quick! I am glad he didn't quit on me.

Dad, Oscar, and I would walk over to Columbus Park for the beginning of our daily regimen. We'd start out with calisthenics. Just when we thought we couldn't do any more, Dad would stop us. He wasn't stopping for a break, but rather to begin the next phase of our workout—running. We'd run so long and hard we thought we were going to die right there in the middle of Columbus Park. Oscar and I would joke that they could just roll our dead bodies next door to Saint Ann's Catholic Church and conduct the funeral! As any athlete knows, these exercises and marathon runs were exactly what we needed to build up our cardiovascular systems and to produce the kind of endurance we would need—especially during those fourth quarters when everyone else was completely exhausted.

Oscar and I would be totally gassed when we finished our run. "That was great!" Dad would exhort. "Now, let's go back to the house and hit those weights!" With that, we'd stumble back to the garage to begin a very detailed weight workout. Mike didn't leave anything to chance with his two disciples. He had a list of exactly what we were to do in weight lifting. The types of lifts, the number of sets and repetitions, everything. He really watched out for us, even when he wasn't physically present. I recall how he would tell us that some days he wouldn't be able to accompany us to our workout but that he would be watching us from his bedroom window. We never knew whether to believe him or not, but we never wanted to run the risk of his seeing us goofing off. So we worked as hard as two guys could. Believe me, there were plenty of warm summer days in 1968 when I was less than grateful for all the work Dad was putting us through, but soon I would understand how valuable it would be.

DEALING WITH A LOSS

I had no idea while I was bench-pressing in the middle of August 1968 in Omaha, Nebraska, that exactly one summer later I would still be bench-pressing, but most everything else would be different. I was no longer in Omaha, but Willcox. I was not as weak as I was in Omaha, having the benefit of twelve months of strength and conditioning workouts. I was no longer a freshman, but now a sophomore. But the biggest change was that I no longer had my coach, my hero, my mentor, my dad.

Mike was gone.

I tried to deal with the loss as best I could. For me, it was a simple strategy of escaping into the world of sports. Fortunately for me, I chose a worthwhile endeavor that would have positive implications for my future. But the same didn't hold true for my dear mother.

Mike's untimely death devastated Mom. She was so shaken by the entire incident that she just didn't know what to do. Unfortunately, she wasn't working, so she sat around Grandma's house with nothing but time on her hands. What started to happen made me angry, but I didn't understand the depths of her despair at the time. Now I understand. I still don't condone what Mom did, but at least I can understand it. In her desperation, Mom turned more and more to alcohol. She was slowly but surely developing a drinking problem that would eventually have to be confronted. But in its beginning, none of us really knew what to do about it. We all just hoped it would go away on its own. I chose to ignore it.

A LOFTY GOAL

Throwing myself into football, I started getting noticed by my teammates, coaches, fellow students, and fans. I can recall being asked about my goals for the future. Even as a tenth grader I was very clear on my direction: "I want to be the first student from Willcox High School to be offered a full athletic scholarship to play football at an NCAA Division I university!"

Even though my goals were certain, which I thought was quite commendable, most folks didn't know what to do with me or my ambitions. The population of Willcox divided itself down the middle in their opinion of this young upstart named Ted DiBiase; half the town thought I was terribly conceited, and the other half of the town thought I was crazy!

It was a difficult time for me. What's more, the man I most wanted to please was gone. But I remembered everything he had said to me. Therefore, I knew the last thing he would have wanted me to do was quit. So I threw myself into football with renewed zeal. It was the only thing that mattered to me.

I reacquainted myself with some of my old friends, but even that was difficult. Because I was so focused on football, I was already achieving some goals that isolated me from my pals. The real strain was produced when I was the only sophomore named to the varsity squad. Of course, this did not sit well with my fellow tenth graders. Added to the loss of Mike was the necessity of dealing with the jealousy of some of my friends.

It was in this context that I began my varsity career with the game of my life that I referred to in the last chapter. At fifteen I was already six feet two inches tall, and weighed 200 pounds. People were starting to notice me, and I thought that was fine—as long as it helped move me toward my goal of a football scholarship at a big school.

That first game in Willcox was incredible. But the bad news was that I would never have another game like it. Our team struggled that season, ending with a disappointing 3-7 record. Nevertheless, I was named to the all-conference first team, as well as all-state honorable mention.

That was a good place to be at the end of the season, and I thanked the Lord that He allowed me to make progress toward my goal. Looking back, it's pretty clear to me now that part of the reason I was excelling was because of my *focus*. I was so clearly locked into sports that no other person, place, or thing mattered. To me, life was all about football.

That was all going to change during the Christmas vacation of 1969.

That's when I met Dixie—my first girlfriend.

A STUMBLING BLOCK

I fell hard for Dixie. It was a different sort of relationship than most kids have when they describe their first love. The major difference was that dear, sweet Dixie lived 150 miles away from Willcox. And neither one of us was old enough to drive at the beginning of our relationship. Yet, in spite of the distance, we dated steadily for a year and a half. (And I had the long distance telephone bills to prove it!)

I was head over heels in love with her, which was a wonderful feeling but did nothing to help me with my focus. Quite frankly, it was the major stumbling block that caused me to lose my focus during that all-important junior year.

Dad had tried to warn me about these things before he died. "Stay focused, Teddy," he told me. "My guess is, the biggest distraction you'll face early in your life will be a girlfriend." I had no idea how well he knew me.

I went into my junior year convinced that I could still play ball as well as ever, even though I had a girlfriend. The townspeople were excited to see what kind of year I was going to have, because I had done so well the year before. There was pressure on me, and I'm afraid I didn't respond to it as well as I could have.

My eleventh-grade football season would probably be best described as "good." It was better than "bad" but a long way from "great." Dixie was indeed creating a distraction that kept me from my best on the field. Ironically, though, the team was turning itself around, and we finished the season at 7-3. But I was in love, so all I could think of was my next trip to see my girlfriend. I was blind to how it was affecting me.

It took my older brother, Mike, to get me to see what was going on. After he graduated from the University of Arizona, Mike joined the military. By the time I was goo-goo gah-gah over Dixie, he was just getting out of the service. He came to Willcox and immediately took me on.

"What are you doing with this girl?" he barked at me.

"Don't worry about me," I replied.

"You're gonna ruin your life," he screamed back in my face, like a marine drill sergeant.

"I'm doing just fine," I continued, in my blind little world.

"What if you get her pregnant?"

"It won't happen."

"You've lost your focus."

A MOTHER AND FATHER REUNION

Mike and I continued to argue for his entire visit. I hated what he was saying. I needed to hear it all, but his manner was so gruff, so abrasive. I couldn't get past his attitude, which really turned me off.

To make matters worse, there was not only pressure from friends, girl-friends, and brothers, but things were getting more difficult at home with Mom. Her drinking was out of control.

My grandmother was doing everything she could think of to pull my mother out of her despair. But, try as she might, nothing seemed to help. It was at that point that Grandma made a call out of desperation. She phoned Ted Wills in Los Angeles.

"Ted, Helen is in really bad shape," Grandma explained. "Nothing seems to help. I thought perhaps you could come out here to visit her. Maybe if she saw you, she might feel a little better."

"Is that a good idea?" Ted stumbled over the phone. "Are you sure she would want to see me?"

"It's worth a try," Grandma answered.

"I don't know…" Ted trailed off.

Grandma felt it was important to add one more thought. "Ted, your son needs a dad."

So Ted Wills returned to Willcox, Arizona, to do what he could to lift my mother out of her depression and to reestablish a relationship with his son. He had better success with my mother than he did with me. It's not that I was unreceptive to Ted, but being in the middle of my teenage years, I had pretty much decided that *no one* was going to take the place of Mike DiBiase in my life. Ted tried, but I knew it wasn't going to happen. I wasn't mean to him, yet I didn't go out of my way to make his life any easier, either.

Instead, he concentrated his efforts on Mom. We were all happy to see her slowly begin to rise out of her drunken depression. She was flattered that Ted had come back to help her. She was responding to him in a way she hadn't responded to anyone in a long time. They enjoyed each other's company. They laughed together. It looked like some old embers were rekindling, and they were.

Eighteen months after Mike DiBiase passed away, my biological father and mother remarried.

STAYING PUT

I was happy for Mom. I had felt so sorry for her in her loss of Mike. Ted Wills came along again in God's exact timing. I was pleased that they could reunite. There was just one issue: I didn't want it to affect any of my goals and future plans. I was fine with everything until the newlyweds announced they were going to move back to Ted's home in Los Angeles, and they expected John and me to go along with them.

It was all right with John, but not OK with me. My mind was already made up. I would stay in Willcox with Grandma and continue my quest to be the first guy from Willcox High School to be awarded a full scholarship to play football at a Division I university. It was too soon for me to have any interest in getting into a new "family." I just wanted to work out, play football, and spend time with my girlfriend. I had worked hard to establish myself in this community, and I didn't want to have to start all over again.

So Ted, Helen, and John packed up all their belongings and rode off into the western horizon in another of my life's strange ironies: Here was my brother going off to be raised by my biological father after I had spent the last ten years being raised by his biological father!

Much later, Ted asked my mother to find out if I would be willing to change my name back from DiBiase to Wills. Mom cautiously approached me on the subject. "What do you think, Teddy?"

"No ma'am," I replied.

"Why not?" she asked.

"It's just not who I am," I answered with all the honesty that was within me. Having been Ted DiBiase for as long as I could remember, I had no animosity toward Ted Wills, but I also had no interest in assuming a new identity. I liked who I was. My parents seemed to understand, because it was never brought up again.

TIME TO REFOCUS

By the summer preceding my senior year it was time for me to get refocused on my goals—or admit that they would go unmet.

God brought a fellow into my life who helped me see how important it was to make the necessary course corrections in order to fulfill my dreams. Robert Lincoln was a friend of my older brother's. He had been recently discharged from the service after fighting as a paratrooper in Vietnam. He was one tough dude, yet he was very easy to talk to. Because his last name was Lincoln, we all called him Abe. I'm not sure why the two of us ended up spending time together, but we had some pretty serious conversations about all sorts of issues.

The more I hung out with Abe, the more I opened up to him, which is something I hadn't done with anybody since Mike's death. It was therapeutic to be able to freely express some of my frustrations to a person who seemed to genuinely care. It didn't take many discussions for me to see that important steps needed to be taken in order for my focus to return. As Abe put it, "Get your mind off the girl and back on football." Eventually, my girlfriend and I broke up. I started working out harder than ever. That's how the summer of 1971 went for me: no more girlfriend, lots of hard work, and a time for refocusing. By the time football season rolled around that fall, I was ready. It paid off too.

God smiled down on me, giving me an outstanding senior season. I was named all-conference at both offensive and defensive tackle. An even bigger honor was being named first-team all-state defensive tackle.

I was very proud of these accomplishments, but deep down inside of me I knew that, even with those honors, it was still going to be a long shot for me to play Division I football.

HITTING THE LONG SHOT

There were plenty of nervous weeks following my senior football season. Each day I would hope to be contacted by some sort of coach, scout, or recruiter. But it was all too quiet for me. Christmas came and went. It became the new year of 1972, and my heart was beating a little harder each new day, not knowing what the future had in store. I had no clue that a January day that began so typically would include such a monumental departure from the norm.

I was sitting in one of my classes that was a required course for all graduating seniors. Seated right in front of me was Kathy Lindsey, one of my best friends over the years in Willcox. She was the closest friend I had in those days. She lived a block away and we went all the way back to second grade together. We were even boyfriend and girlfriend that second grade year! We attended the same church. We were so close that I shared with her my hopes and my dreams.

Trying my best to stay awake in class that day, I hid behind Kathy as the teacher droned on with his lecture. Suddenly, the boredom of the class was interrupted by the principal's voice booming over the loudspeaker: "Ted DiBiase, please report to the main office immediately!"

Kathy turned around and mouthed the words, "What did you do?"

I shrugged my shoulders, clueless as to why I would be pulled from class to go to the office. I somehow managed to extract myself from that tiny desk. Standing up, unfolding my body that had grown to six feet, four inches and 225 pounds, I shuffled down the hall to the principal's office, still uncertain what this was all about. *Am I in trouble?* I thought to myself, as I opened the door. It turned out to be just the opposite.

"Ted, come in, please," the principal beamed, friendlier than I had ever remembered his being.

"Thank you sir," I responded, taking the seat that was waiting for me.

"There's someone here who is very interested in talking to you," the principal continued, pointing to the stranger who was already seated in the other chair. I reached out to shake his hand.

"I'm Ted DiBiase," I introduced myself.

"I know," the man replied. "I am one of the football coaches at the University of Arizona, and I have been sent here to ask you a question..."

My jaw must have dropped to the floor as he continued.

"Would you like to accept a full scholarship to play football at the University of Arizona?"

The principal was grinning from ear to ear. The coach was pretty happy too. I was too dumbfounded to say anything. Finally I found the strength to ask him the big question: "How did you guys know about me?"

The coach smiled and told me an amazing story of how I had come to the attention of the University of Arizona. It was a chain of events clearly orchestrated by the hand of God.

As we had done for years, our family faithfully attended the Catholic church in town. Earlier in the year, the priest who had been in Willcox for years moved to another parish, and a new priest came to our church. Unbeknownst to me, this new priest had come from Tucson, where he was formerly the chaplain of the football team for the University of Arizona.

After seeing me play, he called some of his old friends at the university. "You have to come to Willcox to see this kid play. Take my word for it, your time won't be wasted," he said. So the coaches from the University of Arizona scouted me and liked what they saw.

"We want you at the University of Arizona, son," the coach continued while I sat, still dazed, in the principal's office.

"This is a tremendous honor," the principal gushed, seeing I was in no shape to speak for myself.

"Well, the offer's there, son," the coach concluded. "You think about it. We'll be in touch."

I stood, shook his hand, and somehow made it back to class. As I squeezed back into my desk, Kathy couldn't stand the mystery. She turned around and whispered, "What happened?"

Because she was such a good friend, I knew how to make her understand. "Do you know the dream I've had all these years?"

She nodded.

"Well, it just came to pass!"

"Is there something you would like to share with the entire class, Mr. DiBiase?" my teacher suddenly interrupted.

"I'm sorry, sir," I apologized, realizing I had just disrupted his lecture.

"Well, if you won't, then I will," he replied, to my complete surprise. "Class, Ted has just been offered a full scholarship to play football at the University of Arizona. To my knowledge, this is a first for our little school. Congratulations, Ted!"

With that, the class erupted into applause. Everyone was so happy for me. It was too perfect! In the midst of all my fellow seniors, the goal I had worked so hard to achieve was coming true right before my eyes.

ACHIEVING MY GOAL

It was the most triumphant moment in my life up to that point. I thought of all my classmates who snickered at me behind my back. I recalled all those who made fun of me, saying I had shot too high in my dreams. But they were wrong! This magic moment was my payoff for sticking to my guns all those years.

It was some time after that conversation with the University of Arizona coach that I found out I was chosen to play in the state's North/South football game, which would be held the summer after graduation. It was just one more huge honor, and I took it as a clear sign from God. He had chosen to bless me for my faithfulness to the goal. It was a wonderfully fulfilling time for me.

As my senior year rolled from winter to spring, all was well with my world. I had accomplished my goal, fully intending to sign the letter of intent with the University of Arizona as soon as it was legally possible.

But isn't it funny how life can take a different path from what we intend? And sometimes it all happens so innocently. Like that spring afternoon I was watching television, and the commercial came on announcing that professional wrestling from Amarillo, Texas, was on tour with one of its stops right down the road in Tucson. "I think I'll buy a ticket and go see them," I said to myself. "It would be fun to see some of the old friends we had back in Texas."

That ticket took me somewhere different than I ever expected to go.

7
TURNS IN THE ROAD

It was a calm, sunny day—very typical for Tucson in the late winter and early spring—when I took a trip over to the Tucson Community Center to buy a ticket to see Dad's old wrestling buddies. I had no idea I would see old friends right off the bat on that otherwise normal afternoon.

Once I got inside the arena, I made my way back to the dressing room area. I came up behind Dory Funk Sr. and his son Dory Jr. Tapping them on the shoulder, I said, "Hey, do you guys remember me?"

They turned around and stared at me, looking a bit puzzled. They didn't recognize me immediately, because I had done some growing up since our last time together. But, finally, they recognized me.

I explained to them that I had seen the show advertised on television, so I wanted to come to see them. We all laughed, spending a few minutes recalling fond memories. They asked about my future plans, and I wasn't shy about telling them the good news from the University of Arizona. They seemed especially pleased for my success in the achievement of my goals.

"Where's Terry?" I eventually asked, referring to Dory Sr.'s other son—the member of the family to whom I had been closest.

"He's not with us this trip," his dad responded. "But he'll be here in just a couple of weeks. I'll tell him you were asking for him, so maybe the two of you can get together."

"That'd be super," I replied.

A CHANGE IN DIRECTION?

Two weeks later, my old friend Terry Funk was at the arena in Tucson for the next show. I went back to the dressing room during the show to visit. "It's great to see you, Terry," I said. "I miss some of our old friends back in Texas. How are all of them doing?"

"I was hoping you'd ask that question," Terry answered, a wink in his eye. "There's a way you can find out for yourself."

"What are you talking about?" I asked.

"I'd like to make a suggestion for you to consider," Terry replied, with a hint of mystery in his voice.

"What?" I asked curiously.

"Well," Terry paused, taking a deep breath. "What I would really like to do is get your permission to set you up for a recruiting trip so you can come visit West Texas State just outside of Amarillo. I know for a fact that they'd love to have you on their football team."

"But I've pretty much decided to play football at Arizona," I interrupted in loud protest.

"I know, I know," Terry agreed. "But you haven't had a look at West Texas yet. You may change your mind once you visit us. Plus, you haven't signed your letter of intent yet, have you?"

"Well," I stammered, "I signed a letter to go to Arizona, but it's not the official letter, since it's not National Signing Day yet."

"Good," he said. "Look at it this way, Ted. It'll be a great way to come to town and visit the old gang."

Terry's logic made sense, so eventually he wore me down. *Besides,* I thought to myself, *I'm all set to play for UA, so what's the harm in visiting my old stomping grounds?*

The trip to Amarillo came together quickly. It was so much fun to be back with some of my old friends. They made me feel welcome. It was a homecoming of sorts.

Then I took some time to visit West Texas State out in Canyon, Texas. To my surprise, Terry was right. I liked it more than I thought I would. The coaches knew about the Arizona offer, so they were laying it on thick about how badly they wanted me. The one point they made over and over that I couldn't refute was how much more *personal attention* I would get by attending this, the smaller of the two Division I schools.

Plus, I had a little secret rolling around in the back of my mind. Playing football on scholarship at a major university was a great place to get noticed by National Football League scouts, but I knew it was only the cream of the crop who actually made it to the NFL. What if I didn't get drafted to play pro ball? It was a scenario I had to take seriously. I had given it a lot of thought, and one other direction kept planting itself firmly in my mind: If I didn't make it in pro football, there might be a career in professional wrestling.

Even the thought of it caused me to envision Dad moaning loudly up in heaven, but it was a real desire of mine nonetheless.

The coaches at West Texas were very persuasive. Before I left, I signed a letter of intent, just as I had with Arizona. Neither one was the official commitment letter; but still, it made for one confusing situation for this small-town boy. I went back home not knowing what to do.

A Big Decision to Make

When I returned to Willcox, I was not prepared for the reaction of the towns-people. Word of my recruiting visit to West Texas had leaked out, and there was only one word for the reaction of the people: My visit to West Texas was *scandalous*. Being from a town of die-hard Arizona fans, I should have figured they would have been incensed.

As National Signing Day came closer, the Arizona coaches began putting on some additional pressure. They came to town again, took me out for a nice lunch, and even revealed their secret weapon: "We hear that you might be lean-ing toward West Texas because it would also afford you the opportunity to wrestle. So, we'd like you to meet our very own wrestling coach!"

"Hello, Ted," the coach introduced himself. "We want to be clear that wrestling is also an option at our school."

I left that lunch about as confused as a kid could be. "What should I do, Lord?" I asked God.

Shortly after that luncheon, I was invited to a banquet on campus. "It's a dinner to welcome our incoming freshmen," the coach said over the phone.

"But I still don't know if I want to be one of your incoming freshman," I honestly replied.

"That's OK, Ted. Trust me, you don't have to sign anything. Just come over and enjoy yourself."

The university had asked one of their alumni to drive me to the banquet. Not only was he an alumnus, he was also a former player, as well as a current assistant football coach for the Willcox High School football team. "Ted, you need to be prepared," I recall him warning me. "They will be putting the pressure on you. That's guaranteed."

He was correct. The banquet was a fabulous spread, and they put me up in a very nice hotel. I was living like a king until the next morning when the phone in my hotel room awakened me bright and early at 8 A.M. The call was from a few of the coaches, wanting one last attempt to gain my allegiance.

"Ted, put some clothes on and meet us downstairs for breakfast," the voice on the phone said.

Breakfast was as pressure packed as anything I had ever experienced. "We'll take better care of you than any other school can," they promised. "Think about how great it will be for all your family to be able to come over to Tucson in order to watch you play. All of them won't be making the journey to Amarillo, will they?"

It was at that point that one of the coaches reached inside his jacket and pulled out a carefully folded document. "Ted," he said with great pomp, "we want *you* to be the first person this year to sign the National Letter of Intent to play football for the University of Arizona." With that, he produced a pen and pushed both pen and paper across the table until it was directly in front of me.

"I still don't know," I whispered.

"Ted, come on, just sign it," he prodded. "If you change your mind, we'll rip it up, OK?"

There was something about his last suggestion that finally popped my cork. I got mad, pushed my chair away from the table, and left without signing the letter. I know I was just a high school senior, but I hadn't fallen off the turnip truck. It was a long ride back to Willcox.

West Texas Bound

I didn't have a whole lot of time to think about what had happened, because as soon as I walked into my grandmother's house, the phone rang. "Ted, there's a nice man calling who says his name is Coach Dawson from West Texas State University," Grandma announced. "Actually, this man has been calling here all night."

"Ted, we still want you," he assured me. "You didn't sign with Arizona, did you?"

"No, I didn't sign," I began.

"I can be on a plane in ten minutes. I can come up right now and have you sign the letter of intent that makes it official."

"That won't be necessary, Coach Dawson," I replied, feeling weary of the struggle. "I'm not going to sign with any other school. Just put your letter in the mail. I'll sign it and return it right away."

"Are you sure we don't need to fly over?" he probed, not wanting to lose this deal.

"No, don't worry, I've given you my word. The mail will be fine." With that, my decision was made. I would be attending West Texas State University to study and to play football.

LIFE IN COLLEGE

In the autumn of 1972, I entered West Texas State in Canyon, Texas, as a freshman on a full football scholarship. My college days are years that I now describe as the time that "Ted arrived." As with so many kids who go off to a university, it was a time marked by a gradual departure from my interest in the Lord. Satan was very smart in dealing with me. He didn't throw me off a cliff, but rather he rolled me down a hill. Either way, it was still a fall that landed me at the bottom.

I began justifying behavior that I had never engaged in before. For example, I started drinking beer. I would say to myself, "It's just a part of college life. It's part of being a jock." Unfortunately, one beer led to two, then a six pack. Finish out the picture with my entrance into a notoriously rowdy fraternity, and it's easy to see why this isn't a time that I recall proudly.

STAYING FOCUSED—ON FOOTBALL AND JAYNET

However, upon entering school, I can say that I was still focused on football. At West Texas they had a freshman team that played its own six-game schedule each fall. I started as one of the defensive tackles on a team that ended up winning five and losing one.

After the short season, we worked out with the varsity team, which gave me my first taste of life at that level. It was quite an adjustment, as any collegiate athlete can attest. In high school, you are one of the few superior athletes who rise above all your peers. But once you enroll in college, *everyone is superior.* The dream of playing in the National Football League was being tempered by the reality of all I was up against in college.

It was during the late autumn of my freshman year that I ran into an old friend. It was the young lady who was talking with me in the Amarillo apartment complex the night my dad died. Jaynet Foreman and I went back all the way to sixth grade. She was working in a clothing store in a mall near the school. We went to lunch and relived some old times. Before long, we were dating.

As I look back now, I can see that it was very important for me to have a successful relationship with Jaynet because she was a tangible link to my past. I worked so hard to make her like me that I was initially pretty tense. However, once I started to relax, we really hit it off.

I enjoyed being with her, yet I could still hear my dad's voice ringing in my ears, "Remember, Ted, you can't stay focused with a girlfriend." But I was determined to make it work.

I can also recall a conversation I had with Terry Funk about this time. In the midst of our small talk, he made a very insightful statement: "Ted, you *have* to be with someone. You just can't stand being alone." I hated to admit it at the time, but he couldn't have been more accurate.

My feelings toward Jaynet would run hot, then cold. All I could do was conclude that my doubts were just a normal case of the occasional cold feet. I was in a bad way, not even thinking of praying for God's direction in my feelings about Jaynet. I had virtually stopped attending church.

As my sophomore year began, it was a difficult season in football. Playing only at an average level, I was not good enough to start for the varsity squad. I hated being on the bench, but I had other issues that were more important to me. I guess it would be fair to say that my focus wasn't completely on football that autumn. Why?

Just a few weeks after the season ended, on December 21, 1973, Jaynet and I got married.

MARRIED LIFE AND COLLEGE

Jaynet and I moved into a small off-campus apartment as I finished up the remainder of my second year in college. The summer between my sophomore and junior years, I worked as a lifeguard at a city pool. Now that I was a married man, finances became more important than ever. Fortunately for me, the NCAA changed a rule that very year that would allow me access to a little more money. For years, there had been a restriction against college athletes working in any professional sport of any kind. If you did, you were denied your amateur status, taken out of your given sport, and stripped of your scholarship. But that summer, the NCAA announced that it would be lightening up on that rule so that someone could work in a sport *other* than the sport in which they had their scholarship.

This became important to me because that summer I was offered a job in a professional sport that wouldn't affect my football scholarship. I took a summer job with pro wrestlers in the Amarillo area...as a referee!

INTO THE RING

Without realizing it at the time, I was being prepared to enter a new phase in my life. I had no idea the world of professional wrestling would become so intriguing to me. Every night I would learn a little more about this business. I appreciated the advantage of being the only other person in the ring as two guys would go at it. I had the best seat in the house.

Late in the summer, another event occurred to bring me even closer to my new world. One of the wrestlers got hurt, and a quick replacement was needed. They chose me! Without any pomp or fanfare, I was suddenly thrust into the ring for my first experience as a wrestler. I don't remember anything specific about those first matches, other than the fact that I was green with inexperience. My only hope was to be a fast learner, which I was.

I was having fun, approaching the sport as I had all other athletic pursuits in my life: I gave 100 percent. Not surprisingly, I wasn't very far along in my wrestling career when I partially separated my shoulder. I don't know what hurt more, my shoulder or the fact that I had injured it so close to the beginning of football season. My coach was going to have a fit.

"How could you jeopardize the success of the team by going out and getting yourself hurt?" I could hear him say in the back of my mind. Knowing how angry he was going to be, I decided to lie to him. I told him that I had partially separated my shoulder by falling off a trampoline. That didn't sound so bad.

WORKING THROUGH INJURIES

As my junior year of football began, I worked harder than ever to get myself back into perfect shape. But it wasn't to be. Instead of improving, I was about to endure a Murphy's Law season: Anything that could go wrong for me did go wrong for me.

Early in the season I pulled a hamstring. Not long after, I injured the big toe on my right foot. My buddies on the team began kidding me about all the tape I required before I could even leave the locker room. With my shoulder taped, my hamstring taped, and my toe taped, they started calling me "the Mummy."

The coaches were good to me, trying to work through my injuries with me. One change they had to make was to move me from defensive tackle to offensive tackle. I had lost a step in all this pain, and speed was more vital on the defensive side. It was a good move for me on the one hand—I made the starting team as an offensive tackle, which was no small accomplishment—but I really missed playing on defense. To my way of thinking, defense was the side with all the emotion. I loved the attack on the ball.

My injuries were a big part of my playing that whole season. In particular, my toe did not seem to be healing. The doctors were stumped about the cause until it was eventually discovered why I was in such pain.

"Ted, you've got a case of gout," the doctor announced after examining me in his office.

"Gout?" I replied incredulously. "Isn't that what old people get?"

"Well," he replied with a laugh, "lots of people think that, but gout can affect anyone."

He explained to me that gout is an excess of a particular acid in the body. The excess acid settles into joints in the body. The foot is a common resting place, which explained why my toe was killing me all the time.

When the coach found out what was going on, he felt he had done all he could do. "Go get healed up, Ted," he told me. "Come back to the team when you're feeling better, and we'll take it from there."

Reluctantly and painfully, I had to agree. I was no good to the team in the condition I was in. I ended up missing half of the season, somewhat embarrassed that I wasn't playing because I was trying to get over gout!

PREPARING FOR A COMEBACK

Because I hadn't seen much action during the fall of my junior year, it put even greater pressure on me to look good in spring football. My senior year was directly ahead of me, and I knew people made the autumn squad based on their performance in the spring. So I worked myself as hard as I could.

It paid off. In the spring of my junior year, I regained the starting spot on the varsity squad. It was a good feeling to be back on top in the sport I loved so much. I just knew my dad would be proud of me.

But in a very routine practice that spring, I had one more accident. As I planted my feet to block the defenders, the offensive lineman to my left was blocked into me in such a way that he fell over onto me. I was unable to lift my left foot from its planted position. As we both fell to the ground, I could feel the ligaments stretching in my left knee and an intense, sharp pain in my left ankle.

It could have been much worse, but it was bad enough to bring me back to a place I hated—rehab. I was so discouraged at the thought of all the hours it would take to rebuild my ankle and knee strength. Would it be back to 100 percent by the start of the fall season? Why was all this happening to me?

Looking back now, I find it interesting that when my heart was drawn toward the Lord, my athletic career was almost injury free. But during those wild college days, I went from one bad situation to another.

In the middle of my discouragement, I had a conversation with a guy named Dick Murdock. His dad had wrestled with my dad, and he was a real character. The essence of the conversation centered around one question:

"How would you like to make some really good money this summer?"

8
PAYING MY DUES

"Ted, how would you like to be making $350 every week?" Dick Murdock asked me.

"Wow, that's a lot of money!" I responded.

"You're not kidding," he laughed.

"What do I have to do?" I asked suspiciously.

"Something I already know you enjoy doing," he winked.

"What is it?"

"How would you like it if I could get you a job with the Mid South territory as a wrestler?"

"That sounds great, Dick," I replied excitedly. "Do you think it could really happen?"

"We won't know if we don't give it a try," he answered.

"So, what do I need to do?" I pushed.

Dick thought for a second before replying. "I think you should jump on a plane right away. You need to go to Shreveport, Louisiana, and pay a visit to the man in charge, Bill Watts."

"It sounds good to me," I responded.

Dick and I shook hands, and another chapter in my life's adventure started to take shape.

With that, I went home and told Jaynet of my plans, and I was off to Louisiana to meet with Mid South's premier booker/promoter, Bill Watts.

BACK TO THE RING

I was nervous about the meeting, but Bill treated me very nicely. Knowing only that I was the son of Iron Mike DiBiase and that I was currently playing football on a full scholarship, Bill booked me to wrestle throughout the summer in opening matches all across Louisiana, Oklahoma, Mississippi, and Arkansas.

Having been around the business as much as I was as a kid, I took to the life of a wrestler quickly. I was very fortunate that summer to be working with some great talent who taught me so much about the wrestling world. Guys like

Killer Karl Kox, Harley Race, and Dick Murdock were all there to give me a proper initiation into pro wrestling. It was lots of fun!

Yet, there were difficult issues as well. I made some poor choices at this point in my life, the most significant being the decision to disregard the Lord in the way I was living. I soon fell into a pattern that included traveling to the event, wrestling, checking into the hotel, and heading right off to the bar. Making $350 a week gave me the false confidence that I was some rich, young hotshot. God would just have to take a backseat to my newfound self-dependence.

WHAT ABOUT FOOTBALL?

When I left for Shreveport, I had every intention to make wrestling a summer job only. There was no doubt in my mind that I would return to West Texas State for my senior year. Playing football and graduating were my two goals.

But something happened to me as the summer wore on. I had found something that I knew I could do well, and the money they were paying me was absolutely mesmerizing. Also, I had such a good feeling when I was in the ring. All these positive effects were welling up inside of me.

On the other side of the coin, there was a terrible thought that played over and over in my mind. The scene was of me sitting on the bench for the entire football season because of my injuries.

Everyone who knew me at this point in my life was urging me to return to school for my senior year. It was the logical, rational, objective thing to do. It was a no-brainer.

But I was thinking with a different mind-set. I was thinking like a jock. The realization that my injuries would most likely keep me from playing football, coupled with the love for wrestling that was growing inside of me every day, led to a decision that would have incredible significance in my life.

I called my football coach to tell him I had decided to quit school and pursue my career as a professional wrestler.

Thus, by September of 1975, life had taken a pretty radical turn for the DiBiase family. Instead of being in Amarillo for my senior year, I took Jaynet to a little apartment in Baton Rouge, Louisiana. The move was pretty significant for her because she was required to leave all her friends back in Amarillo. She had spent most of her life there, so this was a real stretch. I tried to be understanding, but I was so distracted with the pursuit of my career, I'm afraid I didn't do a whole lot to help the situation.

To make matters worse, we only had one car, which I would take on the road with me on my trips. She began to feel completely stranded and isolated in that tiny apartment. It didn't take long for her to start climbing the walls in this strange town with no friends and no transportation. Something had to change, or she would go crazy.

A DEMANDING SCHEDULE

We decided to make another move, this time to Shreveport, Louisiana. I was hoping that living in the center of the territory would be a little easier for us to handle. But it didn't help us much, because the schedule was so demanding. Here is what a typical week would look like:

Saturday would begin locally in Shreveport with television spots and interviews for most of the morning.

Then we'd jump in the car and drive approximately three hundred miles to some place like Greenville, Mississippi, for a Saturday night match.

Once the match was over, we'd get back into the car and drive another three hundred miles, almost to Baton Rouge, to a little town called Houma, Louisiana, for a Sunday night match.

On Monday, if we were lucky, we'd be some place close like New Orleans. If we weren't lucky, we'd have to drive another three hundred-plus miles to a place like Tulsa, Oklahoma.

On Tuesday we'd drive another three hundred fifty miles back to Shreveport for a Tuesday evening event.

On Wednesday morning, we would tape more television interviews in Shreveport. We'd eat lunch, climb back in the car, and drive to a new city like Jackson, Mississippi, or Little Rock, Arkansas, for a Wednesday night match.

Thursday night would put us in a town like Greenwood, Mississippi. After the event, we'd drive to Baton Rouge, where we would spend the night.

Friday morning, we were up and off to Lake Charles, Louisiana, another one hundred miles beyond Baton Rouge. We'd wrestle in Lake Charles Friday night, then drag our weary bodies back into the car for the drive back to Shreveport.

On Saturday morning we'd start the whole routine all over again.

Not only was the schedule grueling, but add to it the fact that there were no interstate highways at this time. We did all this driving on small, two-lane back roads throughout the South.

Then there were the traveling conditions. The wrestlers would band together in a carpool, with four or five guys jammed into one car. Carpooling saved us some money and some wear and tear on our cars, but the bad news was the reality of having four or five *huge* guys all crammed into one vehicle.

Each wrestler was responsible to pay his own expenses, which meant we became authorities on cheap motels. Many nights we'd take a room, only to sneak another three guys into it. We'd flip a coin for who would get one of the mattresses on the floor, and the losers got the box springs.

We also had to purchase our own food. There were many evenings we'd raid a local convenience store, buying up loaves of bread and packages of bologna, in order to eat a dinner that was cheap, yet filling. These became affectionately known as "Bologna Blowouts."

MAKING TIME FOR FAMILY

Because of the schedule I maintained, I was barely able to see Jaynet. She was really in a panic, and I knew the move to Shreveport hadn't really helped all that much. Thus, with a little more desperation, we made one more move in an effort to calm my wife. We moved back to Amarillo, Texas, so she could be close to her friends and family. I commuted back and forth to the Mid South region as best as I could. (Think about the schedule I just described, then add trips to Texas on top of it—I told you this world was crazy!)

Of course, this was causing a tremendous amount of strain on our marriage. Not knowing what else to do, we even split up for a while, but eventually we got back together. We were both young, but this sort of stress would have been difficult even for a couple with more maturity. For a full year—from the summer of 1975 through the summer of 1976—I worked in the Mid South, with this wild and wacky form of commuting from west Texas to the venues in the deep South. Something had to change.

By the middle of 1976, I decided to go back to wrestling in the Amarillo territory. This allowed Jaynet and me to rekindle our relationship, which had already grown cold in many ways. In January of 1977, Jaynet announced to me that I was going to be a father that September. We were both excited, not only at the prospect of a baby, but also in the hope that this child might help bring us together in a way that had not been happening for us.

From February through the summer of 1977, I made some contacts with Bob Gigel, Pat O'Connor, and Harley Race, and through them began working in the Kansas City territory. By mid-1977 I was wrestling in both the Amarillo and the Kansas City territories. Just like my father before me, I was learning that part of the key to success in this business was avoiding overexposure in any given territory. It was a demanding time in my life and far from glamorous, but it was what a young wrestler had to endure in order to pay his dues.

A TITLE SHOT

In September of 1977, my son Michael was born in Amarillo.

The birth of my son would be used as part of the story line to build up to the most significant match in my young career. Harley Race was the world champion at that time, so we set up a world title match in which I would wrestle him.

Harley, remember, is the guy who tried to save my dad's life at ringside. The wrestling fans knew that fact, which made the match between Harley and me even more intriguing.

In order to publicize the event, I was interviewed on television. Appropriately enough, I came to the interview with my new son cradled in my arms. The interviewer got to the heart of the matter right off the bat: "Ted, why do you want to be the heavyweight champion?" he asked, jamming the microphone in my face.

"Well," I began, looking down at Michael. "There are lots of reasons why I want to be the heavyweight champion, but I am holding the most important."

"And who is that you're holding?" he asked.

"This is my son, Michael. He is my father's namesake. I want to be the father to him that Iron Mike was to me."

That was all I had to say. It struck a chord with the fans of Amarillo. The event sold out!

The match gave the fans their money's worth too. We wrestled to a one-hour time-limit draw. In today's world of fast-paced TV sound bites, two guys in a ring for sixty minutes battling to a draw is a foreign concept. But Harley and I put on a show, to be sure. I was grateful that Harley was the kind of guy who did whatever he could to make a young wrestler like me look good.

DIFFERENT TERRITORY, SAME SCHEDULE

Life in the Amarillo territory allowed me to be closer to Jaynet and Michael geographically, but it was every bit as demanding as the Mid South region.

Here is what a typical week looked like for me in 1977:

Saturday morning was reserved for local television taping in Amarillo. Then, we'd get in a carpool for a three-hundred-fifty-mile trip to Colorado Springs or Pueblo, Colorado.

Saturday night we'd wrestle in Colorado. After the match, we'd drive to Albuquerque, New Mexico, another three hundred fifty miles. We'd arrive in the middle of the night, find a motel, and flip a coin for the mattresses.

Sunday morning we'd have live interviews in Albuquerque on its local television station.

Sunday night we'd wrestle in Albuquerque, then jump back in the car for a drive back to Amarillo. Thus, Saturday and Sunday would see us put nine hundred miles on our cars (and our bodies).

On Monday, we would drive to Abilene, Texas, about two hundred sixty miles away, for an evening match.

After the match, we'd drive a hundred miles in the middle of the night on our way to Odessa, Texas.

We'd wrestle in Odessa Tuesday night, cram ourselves into the car, and log another hundred miles over to San Angelo, Texas.

Wednesday night we'd be in San Angelo for a match. Upon its conclusion, we'd drive three hundred miles to get back home to Amarillo before the sun came up on Thursday.

Thursday night was reserved for wrestling locally in Amarillo.

On Friday, we'd drive one hundred miles to Lubbock, Texas, for a Friday evening match. When it was over, we'd drive back to Amarillo, climb into bed for a few hours of much-needed sleep before beginning the routine all over again with television taping on Saturday morning.

It was a wild ride, to say the least. The miles we put on our cars took their toll as well. The first car I owned as a wrestler was a 1975 Ford Gran Torino. The first year it was mine it was always jammed full of wrestlers, and I put more than sixty thousand miles on it. Like it or not, we were in a situation where a new car was necessary just about every two years. And, of course, no one provided that car for us. The money came out of our own pockets.

Those were clearly years of learning for me. I was following the path all wrestlers must take in order to move up the ladder. I was paying my dues, earning my stripes. And, like any other wrestler who is put through this process, I became very hungry to move up to the next level. I really wanted to be on the card as the main event. But things like that don't just happen because we want them to.

I needed a big break.

9
MY FIRST BIG BREAK

To be a professional wrestler, you've got to really love what you do. There's a routine that becomes painfully boring if you're not committed to your craft. Most days looked like this:

Travel to a city.
Work the show.
Eat.
Rest.
Work out.
Travel to the next show.

It was a life of Bologna Blowouts and driving late at night on terrible roads with a group of guys who probably already had drunk a few too many beers. God was certainly watching over us during those demanding days. It was a miracle there were no auto accidents on those scary back roads. Yet, no matter how you viewed it, we were working hard.

I guess that's why it bothers me to this day when people ask me the question: "Is professional wrestling real or fake?" I get upset with that question because of the use of the word *fake*. To me, *fake* gives the impression that the job of a wrestler is easy. Believe me, it's far from easy.

Wrestling is a sport and it's theater as well. To be an effective professional wrestler you need the winning combination of being an athlete and an entertainer. That's part of why it takes so long to learn the business. To be skilled enough to be main-event talent usually takes five to seven years of working before a crowd night after night.

THAT'S ENTERTAINMENT!

It's more than coincidental that some of the people who appreciate what we do the most are other entertainers. Years after I had made it in wrestling, I was hired to be part of a movie called *Paradise Alley*, starring Sylvester Stallone. The script called for a montage depicting one of the main characters in the movie wrestling a variety of opponents. They brought in a bunch of us pro wrestlers to film the various scenes in the ring.

While we were shooting our scenes, many of the Hollywood extras sat off to the side and took turns poking fun at what they were observing. We were just doing our stuff, so we tried to stay out of trouble. (Believe me, it was tempting to go over there and deck a few of them!) The laughing and cutting comments continued until one person in particular had enough.

It was Sylvester Stallone.

Angrily he raised his voice at the group of extras: "I don't want to hear any more cute remarks about these wrestlers," he barked. "What these guys will do in three days would take you Hollywood extras *two weeks!*"

That shut them up!

"I believe that these wrestlers are the best improvisational actors in the business," he concluded.

That sure made us feel good!

So, are we entertainers? You better believe it.

But are we athletes as well? Absolutely!

And do we ever get hurt? Yes. Wrestling takes an incredible toll on your body over time.

But I am getting ahead of myself. There was still a long road ahead for me before I was able to stand on a Hollywood movie set with Sylvester Stallone.

Making Myself a Name

Jaynet, Michael, and I were still living in Amarillo as 1977 came to a close. Beyond wrestling in the Amarillo area, I had picked up some more exposure by going in and out of the Kansas City territory. Of course, the two big venues in that section were Kansas City and St. Louis.

I was slowly making a name for myself. Guys who were in a position to help me were trying their best to put me in the right situation. I'm sure many of the men who helped me early in my career did so, at least in part, because they had been friends with my dad. But the way I looked at it, they were like the quarterback handing the ball off to me. It wasn't enough just to get the hand-off. Now it was time for me to run with the ball.

And, I hoped, to get a big break along the way.

Early in 1978, my first big break came. My name came to the attention of Sam Mushnick, the promoter in St. Louis. He came up with the idea that would give me more exposure than I had received up to that point.

Because wrestling was still regional at this point, the closest thing to a national organization was the National Wrestling Alliance, or NWA. The NWA would crown a world champion who would travel from region to region defending his title against regional challengers. In 1978, the NWA heavyweight champion was my father's old friend, Harley Race. Sam had an idea that included me.

"What if you were to wrestle Harley Race for a shot at the NWA championship?" Sam Mushnick asked me one day.

"That would be fantastic!" I replied.

"Great. So let's try to make it happen," he said.

"What do I need to do?" I asked eagerly.

"Well, in order to have a shot at Harley, you would have to be the Missouri state champion. That should be your most immediate goal. If that happens, you'd be first in line to challenge Harley during his next swing through St. Louis. Are you up to it, my boy?"

"Yes sir!" I answered.

So, early in the spring of 1978, in front of a sellout crowd at the famous Kiel Auditorium in St. Louis, the main event featured a young Ted DiBiase slated as the challenger against the NWA world heavyweight champion, Harley Race.

A SHOT AT THE TOP

The match was filled with excitement, as well as strong symbolism for me. Here I was, wrestling the man who had worked so hard to resuscitate my father ten years before, and now he was doing his part to ensure that I would be noticed in my first big break in the business.

Harley and I wrestled to a one-hour time-limit draw, so he maintained his championship belt. But even the most dedicated fans got a match that didn't disappoint.

I didn't beat Harley Race that night, but something better happened. I got the exposure I desperately needed to move to the next plateau as a wrestler. I knew that if I was good enough to succeed in St. Louis, doors would open to other cities in the United States, and those doors would lead to a great future for a young wrestler with promise.

So I was thrilled beyond words when I was told that another promoter was interested in my services. It would be an important career step for me. The man inquiring about my availability was Mr. Vince McMahon Sr. He ran the wrestling region hubbed in New York City, called the World Wrestling Federation. The WWF wasn't national yet, but it was powerful.

MOVING ON TO THE BIG TIME

Vince McMahon found out about me through Sam Mushnick. New York was known at that time as "Big Body Territory." Because I was still a young kid who was not very big when measured by wrestling standards, I didn't think I had much of a chance to get hired by the WWF.

New York was the home of some of the biggest guys in the business. We're talking about guys like these:

Bruno Sammartino

Pedro Morales

Ivan Putzky

Captain Lou Albano

Chief Jay Strongbow

Gorilla Monsoon

Superstar Billy Graham (not the Reverend!)

It was pretty heady stuff for me even to be considered in the same league with these men.

Also, the WWF would afford me the opportunity to wrestle in some of the most incredible venues in the country. I closed my eyes, trying to imagine what it would feel like to be in a ring in Madison Square Garden in New York City. Or the Boston Garden. Or the Spectrum in Philadelphia. Or the Cap Center in Washington, D.C. It was as exciting a possibility as I could have ever imagined.

God was smiling down on me, even though I had foolishly come to a place where I wasn't looking up at Him. My hope was realized, and by the end of 1978 I was about to begin working for the WWF. We loaded up all our stuff and moved the family to a suburb outside of New York City, across the river in northern New Jersey.

The move to the WWF was a big one for me professionally. There was more money, more prestige, more exposure. Jaynet would have the same adjustment problems that had plagued us when we first left Amarillo several years earlier, but I was hoping that this time it would be different. Unfortunately, it wasn't.

WRESTLING OVEREXPOSURE—AGAIN

I wrestled in the WWF for about a year before the issue of overexposure raised its head again. During that year, however, I gained some valuable contacts that would help later in my career, not the least of which was the connection with the McMahon family.

One of the most enjoyable aspects of that year was traveling with an old buddy of mine, Merced Solis, known in the wrestling world as Tito Santana. He and I had played football together at West Texas State. The old tight end and I had great fun together as a tag team in many matches during that year.

A significant moment came toward the end of that year, 1979. A young kid showed up from Tampa, Florida, and got the attention of Vince McMahon Sr. Vince took one look at the kid's incredible physique, deep tan, and long blond hair, and saw dollar signs in a big way.

My last match with the WWF in Madison Square Garden was against this new kid. It was his first time to wrestle in the Garden, but we all knew he was destined for greatness. To us, he was Terry, but he would quickly explode onto the scene in his new persona, Hulk Hogan.

As Hulk began to establish his identity in New York, it was time for me to move along in order to avoid the dreaded wrestling disease known as overexposure. I linked up once again with Bill Watts Sr. As the decade of the '70s ended, I rented a U-Haul trailer and moved my wife and son with me to Baton Rouge, Louisiana, for another stint in the Mid South region.

OUR BREAKUP

New York had been good for us as a family because the region was more compact, so I was home more. But once we moved to Baton Rouge, Jaynet saw that an old pattern was emerging. I was going to be on the road more than ever. I knew she wasn't happy in our marriage, and it continued to deteriorate. I wasn't happy with the situation either. I just didn't know what the answer was.

I was talking on the phone one evening with my mother when she brought up the subject of my miserable situation. "Ted," she advised, "look yourself in the mirror and answer one question, 'Do I love this woman?'" I realized the answer was no.

After the next road trip, I came home and made a radical suggestion to Jaynet. "I think it might be a good idea if we separate for a while," I said. Not surprisingly, she completely agreed.

On a winter day in early 1980, Jaynet and Michael got on an airplane to Amarillo. I tried to act brave and strong, but one of the hardest things I have ever done in my life was put those two on that plane. When I said good-bye to Michael, it almost killed me.

I went back to the empty apartment in Baton Rouge a devastated man. I knew it was over for Jaynet and me. It was a horrible price to pay for two people who couldn't stay married. The pain of losing my son was almost unbearable.

Jaynet and I never reunited. Shortly after that plane trip to Amarillo, we were divorced. I was sad, lonely, and discouraged. Professionally, things were moving along, but personally, I was a mess. I had drifted so far away from the Lord, I didn't even know how to return to Him.

I continued to wrestle in the Mid South region, not knowing if I would ever meet someone whom I could love and trust and who would feel the same way about me. I didn't know what to do. But God did.

10
MELANIE

I gave the Mid South region another six months of my life, but by the summer of 1980, I decided it was time for another change. My career goal was to get the kind of exposure I needed to be considered as the next candidate for the National Wrestling Alliance championship. It wasn't happening in Baton Rouge, but I had an idea where it could happen: Atlanta.

I started working for Georgia Championship Wrestling that summer. Because it was covered by television station WTBS, it was a move filled with lots of important possibilities. It didn't hurt my future that WTBS was owned by a guy named Ted Turner either!

My first "home" in Atlanta was an apartment complex called The Falcon's Rest. It was seedier than it sounds, and I couldn't think of any falcon that would live in a place that bad. I'm glad I was on my own at that time in my life, because it was no place for a wife or a son. I pretty much kept to myself, except for my wrestling buddies, like Terry Taylor.

Another one of the guys I traveled with at the time was my friend Steve Kern. He had a wife and a new baby, and he lived in a much more desirable part of the greater Atlanta area—a pleasant community, north of the city, known as Stone Mountain.

"Ted, you've got to get out of that dump of an apartment and move up to Stone Mountain," Steve would persist, as we were out on the road somewhere driving to another match. "Yeah, I know," I'd answer, but not feeling really motivated to do anything about it.

"Well then, DO IT!" he said, pounding his fist on the steering wheel in frustration.

He badgered me for months. Thanks to his persistence, by the spring of 1981, I was ready to make one more move. I ended up at the Summit Creek apartment complex in Stone Mountain. Looking back, it was one of the most significant moves I have ever made.

Getting a Tan—and Much More

I hit the Georgia Championship Wrestling circuit as hard as I could. One of my favorite angles was the time I was "injured" in a match, requiring me to spend a week in a local Atlanta hospital. The name of the hospital was announced on WTBS during the event—it wasn't meant to be much of a secret—so I was entertained by a steady stream of mail, flowers, and visitors.

In only seven days, I was released from the hospital. The fans were patiently waiting because I was due to make my comeback a month later in a big match in Atlanta's Omni Arena.

The Sunday after my week in the hospital was a warm, sunny April day, a perfect day for working on my tan. I called several of my friends to join me, but most were already busy. LuAnn, the girlfriend of one of my buddies, was available, however, so we met down by the swimming pool in the center of the apartment complex.

I was reclining at poolside in my chaise lounge, working on my monster tan, when I spotted the most beautiful girl I had ever seen.

The importance of my tan took a backseat to my fascination with this woman. I watched her all day. LuAnn, aware that I was transfixed by this beauty finally asked, "Ted, what's going on?"

"I'd really like to meet *her!*" was all I could say in response, as I pointed toward the beautiful blond in the bikini.

Well, to my disappointment, it didn't happen. LuAnn and I packed up our things and returned to our apartments later that afternoon. I sat in my apartment, overcome with a restless, antsy feeling.

I had to come up with some sort of creative plan to get back around this young woman. *Maybe there's an outside chance I could meet her if I went back down by the pool,* I reasoned to myself. *I know—I'll go back down, pretending that I lost something that I need to look for!* I was so proud of my little scheme. I just hoped it would work.

It did.

I was only there a short time before one of the guys this woman was hanging out with came over to me with a request: "Ted, there's a young lady over there who would really love to have your autograph."

And with that, he pointed directly at the woman I wanted to meet. At that point, I realized he was playing a joke on her, but nonetheless I immediately turned on the charm.

"Well, come on over here," I beckoned, being as cool as I could. "I'll be glad to give you an autograph."

Shyly she walked toward me.

"I'm Ted," I smiled, introducing myself.

"Hi, I'm Melanie," she replied. "Melanie Kennedy."

"What would you like me to sign?" I asked.

Realizing she didn't have any paper, she took off a visor she was wearing. "Could you sign this for me?"

"Sure thing," I responded, trying to play as smoothly as I could. I located a pen and started to sign the visor, but I discovered that it was so wet the pen wouldn't write on its surface.

"This isn't working," I announced. Suddenly, I had an even better idea. "Why don't you follow me back to the manager's office and I can give you a real autograph on a piece of paper."

"OK," she answered, and she followed me over to the manager's office.

I was so excited! I thought I was so cool! Everything went great until she asked me an unusual question: "So, what's it like to be an Atlanta Falcon?"

I froze. I just looked at her, but I could tell by her expression she wasn't kidding. Melanie didn't know I was a wrestler. She thought I was a professional football player, because a lot of the players lived nearby.

I swallowed hard and explained to her that I wasn't a part of the NFL but a part of Georgia Championship Wrestling.

"You're a *wrestler?*" she asked incredulously.

By then we were at the office. I found a piece of paper, and scribbled down the following words: *To Mel, The best looking girl at the pool, for sure.* Then, in an attempt to be cute, I signed it, "Love, Ted DiBiase."

(By the way, we still have that autographed piece of paper. It's now beautifully framed and hangs in a prominent place in my office. I have to admit, it's the most important autograph I have ever given.)

As I handed the paper to Melanie, I continued my cute routine. "This is gonna cost you," I remarked.

"What do you mean?" she asked.

"I would like your phone number, so I could call you sometime," I replied, still desperately trying to be cool.

"Well, I don't usually give out my phone number," she answered.

But God smiled down on me. I got it.

The very next day I was back down at the pool, in the hopes I would see Melanie again. She had mentioned the day before that she might be back down there, so I knew it was where I wanted to be. For some reason, there were a lot more people at the pool this time than the previous day. I scanned the entire area—and it was a huge pool area—but I didn't see her anywhere.

The pool was actually a two-level construction with a fountain and a hot tub and all that sort of stuff. I decided the best place for me to see everything was sitting on the side of the pool on the top level. I had a perfect view of the whole complex, but I still couldn't find Melanie.

However, from my lookout post I observed three attractive young women swimming down in the lower level, so I decided to get them to notice me by diving into the pool. I guess I was pretty impressive, for when I resurfaced, I had their attention. I was about to begin some serious flirting when I met eyes with one of the three women. To my utter amazement, I hadn't recognized this particular young lady.

It was *Melanie!*

I was embarrassed beyond description. She thought the whole scene was quite humorous, but I was really feeling foolish. Fortunately, it didn't take long to feel comfortable in her company.

OUR FIRST DATE

We spent the entire day together at the pool. We talked and laughed and just enjoyed one another's presence. I learned about her family background and her upbringing, and the more I learned, the more I liked. As the day was ending, I asked her if she would go out to dinner with me. We went to Benihana, the Japanese restaurant nearby, and had a great time.

I didn't want the evening to end. I guess Melanie felt the same way. "I know a really fun place to go dancing," she said. "Would you like to go?"

"Yeah! That sounds terrific," I answered. Anything to spend a little more time with her.

I paid the dinner check and we headed off in my car to the dance club. On the way there, Melanie made an odd observation: "Oh, by the way, Ted, you will probably be the oldest person at this dance club, just so you can be prepared!"

"I'm only twenty-six!" I responded. "I'm sure I won't be that much older than everyone."

"OK."

We rode in silence for a while, but that comment got me thinking. I know a guy isn't supposed to ask these sorts of questions, but now I was really curious. "Melanie, how old are you?"

"Nineteen."

"Nineteen?" I repeated.

"Yes." She turned to look straight at me, but I never took my eyes off the road. Finally, she asked the question that was on her mind. "Ted, just how old did you think I was?"

I tried to word my answer carefully. "You look older than nineteen," was all I could think of to say. "I mean that as a compliment," I added.

She smiled and then we both started laughing. Before long, we arrived at the dance club. We had a fun time, but Melanie was absolutely correct. I was the oldest person in the place.

SPENDING TIME TOGETHER

It was an unusual time in my wrestling career because almost all of the wrestling I was involved in took place in the state of Georgia. I was home a lot more than I had ever been. It was the perfect scenario, because I was able to see Melanie just about every day.

We were falling in love. People do crazy things when they're dating. I can remember having to be on the road in Ohio for an event when Melanie had also left town to go to Mississippi to visit her family. She returned to Atlanta the night I was wrestling in Columbus, Ohio. I called the airline to book a flight back to Atlanta, because I wanted so badly to see her. The agent told me the last flight of the day back to Atlanta was only a few minutes after I was scheduled to wrestle. "Book me on that flight!" I bravely informed the agent. "I'll make it."

And I did. Of course, I was still dressed in my wrestling paraphernalia, drenched with perspiration, and looking like an escapee from the local mental asylum. But I made it. And I had any seat on the plane I wanted.

It really was a good time, but it did have its share of confusion. We were getting along wonderfully, and it was getting serious. Melanie would think in her quiet moments, *I'm falling for a professional wrestler! Plus, he is so much older than I am! This isn't how I imagined it would be.*

Our families were against it as well. "He hasn't even been divorced all that long," Melanie's parents would lovingly point out to her. "We're just saying you'd better be very careful."

But there was one bright spot on the family scene. Around this time in our dating, I invited my grandmother from Arizona to visit in Atlanta. She came to town, and I immediately introduced her to Melanie. I valued her opinion highly, so I was delighted that she fell in love with Melanie almost instantly. The three of us had a fabulous time sightseeing around Atlanta. It was a wonderful sight to see my grandmother wander wide-eyed around Underground Atlanta so happily, and, of course, the time together only endeared Mel to me even more.

Leaving Melanie

To further complicate things, while my personal life was going along so well with Melanie, the Mid South region was really putting the pressure on me to leave Atlanta in order to return to their venues. I didn't know what to do. It was going OK with Georgia Championship Wrestling, but the folks at Mid South were making it sound even better there.

With very mixed feelings, I moved back to Baton Rouge, Louisiana. Melanie was such a wonderful support that she even helped me move. As soon as I relocated, I had a television spot I had to do in Shreveport. Leaving Melanie surrounded by a stack of boxes in a bare apartment, I hustled off to my appointment. In the short time I was gone, Melanie set up my entire apartment all by herself—much better than I could have done, I must add. This woman was something special.

It was a sad moment when I watched her board the plane to fly back to Atlanta. I was miserable without her. I tried everything to get my mind off her, but nothing worked. We both missed each other terribly. Our plan to live in separate cities lasted only two weeks.

"Mel, I need you to come back down here and be with me," I pleaded with her on the phone.

"Where will I live?" she asked.

"You can move in with me," I responded.

Neither of us was completely comfortable with this idea. We had both been brought up to understand that living together outside of marriage is not

God's will for us. Melanie's parents were both shocked and disappointed when she agreed to come down.

Looking back, I now know exactly what was going on in my mind. I'm not advocating living together outside of marriage, so make no mistake about that. But I was scared. I knew I loved Melanie. I knew I wanted to marry her. But I didn't want to marry her until she knew exactly what she was getting into. I saw the toll that life with a professional wrestler took on my first wife. I just couldn't do this to Mel without her having a deeper, fuller understanding of my life as a wrestler.

FOXY'S HEALTH CLUB

Melanie was a complete stranger to the town of Baton Rouge. She didn't know a single person, and the only social connections either of us really developed at that time came through the health club we both joined. It was run by a wonderful guy named Foxy, and it was appropriately called Foxy's Health Club. It would prove to be incredibly instrumental in our lives.

Foxy's Health Club was more than a place where we worked out, played racquetball, met friends, and hung out. Although the club was important to both of us, Melanie particularly thrived in this environment. She was able to make some wonderful acquaintances there. One girl in particular, Chilon Humphreys, would become her dearest friend, even to this day.

The other part of this health club story was unfolding in God's perfect time. It didn't take long for us to discover that Foxy himself was more than just a wonderful man. He was also a deeply committed Christian! He had a heart for reaching all who were in his world, and part of that outreach was a voluntary weekly Bible study at his home for his employees and guests.

Chilon invited Melanie to join her at Foxy's Bible study, and the two of them became deeply involved in it. I wanted to be a part of it, but my work schedule was so demanding that I had no time to join in.

I had a deep respect for Foxy, and he was very good at being able to tell folks what God said about the issues of life.

Because Melanie was plugged into this Bible study, we became increasingly uncomfortable living together. We decided to go to Foxy for some counsel. He was the perfect blend of compassion and firmness. He helped us to see that marriage was God's design, which of course, we both already knew. He provided the opportunity for Melanie to discuss the many issues that she had to resolve. And for me, in particular, Foxy helped me see that God would get me past the fears that I was bringing into this relationship from my previous marriage. This crazy health club owner proved to be God's man at God's time. It was remarkable how valuable Foxy's counsel was to both of us at that time in our lives.

We decided to get married. In the midst of our excitement, we laughed when Melanie gave a prediction concerning her family's reaction: "Ted, my mother's gonna kill me!"

But we knew we were doing the right thing. It was appropriate that Melanie and I had a small wedding a short time later at Foxy's house. On New Year's Eve, December 31, 1981, we were married.

"Uncle Sam" DiMaria performed the ceremony. We met Sam through Chilon's husband, Randy Humphreys, and Foxy. Among his many ministry pursuits, Uncle Sam had a weekly Christian television program geared to the children in Baton Rouge. Because he was such a close, personal friend to all of us, it seemed natural and comfortable to have him officiate the ceremony in Foxy's home.

Melanie's maid of honor was Shari Daggett, and my best man was Sylvester Ritter, better known to all wrestling fans as Junkyard Dog. My son, Michael, all of four years old, was part of our ceremony as well.

ADJUSTING TO MARRIAGE—AND FATHERHOOD

The first few months after our wedding found Melanie and me adjusting quite nicely to married life. We moved into a nicer apartment complex in the Baton Rouge area, we were enjoying our new friends, and the wrestling business was going well. And we were still attending Foxy's Bible study, which was continuing to prod us in the right direction spiritually.

About three months into our marriage we realized there was a precaution we were not exercising. "Ted, I think I better make an appointment with the doctor for him to prescribe me some birth control pills," Melanie mentioned one day.

"Sure, Mel. Whatever you think is best."

The day came for Melanie to visit her physician. I remember the day well, because I was sick as a dog with some sort of flu or virus that made me tired, weak, and unable to keep anything down. Melanie didn't feel too well that day, either, which she casually mentioned to her doctor. He checked her over, but was frustrated because he couldn't find any reason to explain her discomfort. As a last resort, he suggested a pregnancy test. Mel laughed as they went through the appropriate procedures.

The doctor was laughing when he returned with the results. "It looks like we are a little too late with that birth control prescription!"

Melanie was in shock. Her first words? "My mother is gonna kill me…all over again!"

She returned home to her sick wrestler, who was horizontal on the couch, doing his impersonation of a dishrag.

"TED, I'M PREGNANT!" she screamed as she entered our place.

Too sick to fully understand the significance of what she was saying, I simply put my hand on her knee and patted it weakly. "You'll be OK, honey," was all I could say.

Looking back, I don't think that was very comforting.

11
THE CREATION OF
THE MILLION DOLLAR MAN

On November 8, 1982, Melanie went into labor. Soon after, my second son was born in Baton Rouge, Louisiana.

We decided to call him Teddy.

The birth of a child is a wonderful time of family rejoicing, as it was in our case. Melanie and I were both trying our best to make our marriage successful. I was haunted by the failure of my first marriage, knowing how much of it was directly related to the life of a professional wrestler. We knew it was going to take work on both of our parts, so we were giving it the best we had.

Yet I was still drifting spiritually. I was living a life that was self-centered and self-absorbed. I had no place for God in my life, which was so foreign from how it had been when I was younger. The next few years would provide a slow but steady erosion that would eventually catch up with me.

I was wrestling in the Mid South region for Bill Watts. Back up in the WWF, Vince McMahon Sr. passed on the baton of leadership to his son, Vince Jr. We didn't realize it at the time, but young Vince would start changing the face of wrestling in a fairly dramatic way. Meanwhile, down south it was time for me to shake things up in my own career. The opportunity arrived right before Teddy's birth.

FROM GOOD GUY TO VILLAIN

In the language of the wrestler, there are two types of characters in the ring: a baby face and a heel. Obviously, one is a good guy, the other a villain. Up to 1982, I was unmistakably a baby face. During my days in the Mid South, one of the guys I wrestled was my best friend and best man at my wedding, Junkyard Dog. He was also a baby face. Everybody loved this big, black tower of strength. Junkyard Dog was so popular in the region that when a survey was conducted in New Orleans concerning the most popular sports figures, Junkyard came in first, with second place going to the *New Orleans Saints!*

Talent constantly changed in the region as wrestlers moved in and out. At that time, Bill Watts and his associate, Ernie Ladd, were looking for a new heel. "Keep your eyes open, Ted," they would say to me.

"What are you looking for?" I asked.

"We're looking for a guy to become the perfect heel."

I promised them I would check things out, which I did. Every night from that point on, I would observe the talent in the Mid South, looking for the next quintessential heel.

One day, while we were wrestling in Shreveport, I found the guy. After the event, I ran excitedly to Ernie's hotel room and started pounding on the door. "What's going on, Ted?" he asked.

"I found our heel!" I announced triumphantly.

"Great!" he responded. "Who is he?"

"You're looking at him!"

Ernie's eyes were as big as basketballs. "Are you kidding?"

"No, I'm serious. This could be a great move!"

"You?"

"Me!"

Apparently, the more Ernie thought about it, the more he liked it. He passed on the idea to Bill, who thought it was fabulous. The story line was a natural: The two close buddies, Ted DiBiase and Junkyard Dog, have a falling out. The two baby faces have a disagreement that causes one to turn on the other.

It was perfect! But would the fans go for it?

The answer was a resounding yes! The feud between Junkyard Dog and me created one of the biggest money-making scenarios ever recorded in Mid South wrestling history.

I was thrilled over the notoriety I received for being such a good heel. It was a great time for me professionally. I started blossoming as a talent, due in large part to Bill Watts. He was not an easy man to work for, but I learned so much from him about the *why* and the *how* of the wrestling business.

The added success was a two-sided coin. On one side, there was a lot of money, more than I had ever made. The other side was the incredibly heavy demand that was put on my time. Bill would always refer to it as "the nature of the beast." But the beast was getting the best of me. And I was still afraid of what might happen to my wife and young son.

TIME FOR ANOTHER CHANGE

By the beginning of 1983, I had all I could take at Mid South. *I need some time off,* I concluded to myself. *I have a new wife and a new son. If I'm not careful, I will fall into the same pattern I was in with Jaynet and Michael.* It was no fun for Melanie in Baton Rouge, so a move had to take place. I chose to go back to Georgia Championship Wrestling, reasoning that the move to Atlanta would be good for me, and especially good for Melanie. Putting her back in her old stomping grounds, surrounded by her friends, would be just what she needed to survive with a husband in this business.

Bill Watts was less than enthusiastic about my plans to leave. Having put so much support behind my new heel character, he was not pleased with my timing. "You're leaving money on the table," he said, rolling his eyes and shaking his head in disbelief. His look told me a lot more could have been done with my new character. Nonetheless, I had to move. Maybe this bad-guy image could be cultivated further in a future setting, but I had to make a change now.

So Melanie, Teddy, and I packed up our things and moved to Clarkston, Georgia, a quaint little town just outside of Atlanta. I had high hopes that this would be the perfect setting for my wife and son. But the saying "You can never go back home," rang painfully true in our situation. All of Melanie's friends were at different places in their lives, as was Mel. The carefree, cute teenager had become a twenty-year-old married mother. The differences were significant enough for things to be somewhat strained.

So much for the perfect move.

LOSING MY MOM

That Christmas, I invited my mother to come out for a visit. Teddy was just over a year old when Mom came to Atlanta from Arizona. She had only been with us a few days when she became quite ill, requiring us to hospitalize her at nearby Piedmont Hospital. The doctors told us she had bronchitis and emphysema, as well as a host of other maladies related to her drinking problem. It was too much for Mom to overcome.

She never left that hospital. She died March 4, 1984.

BACK TO THE MID SOUTH

As 1984 wore on, Ted Turner and Vince McMahon agreed to a deal that would put the WWF on TBS, Turner's nationwide cable channel. This could have been a good thing for me, but as it turned out, I was starting to feel a bit "squeezed out" by the new presence of the WWF in Atlanta.

Fortunately, over the previous few years, I had been cultivating a good relationship with the major wrestling promoters in Japan. I was visiting Japan three or four times a year, doing shows all over the country.

But it wasn't enough without an American base. Late in 1984, Melanie and I decided it would be a good idea for me to return to Bill Watts at Mid South—except this time we would move to a new location. Melanie's parents had relocated near Jackson, Mississippi, so we decided to move near them. We left the suburbs of Atlanta in October of 1984, and in early 1985 we bought our first home in a beautiful town right outside of Jackson, called Clinton, Mississippi. That wonderful little town has remained our home to this day.

Going back to Mid South worked out well professionally, as Bill Watts was more than willing to rekindle our relationship. I jumped right back into my status as a world-class heel. I wrestled in the Mid South for all of 1985 and 1986.

It was a good time for us in many ways. Melanie was more comfortable than I had seen her in quite some time. Being near her parents gave her some support and encouragement, plus it provided her parents with close access to their new grandson. I was grateful because I had not been my in-laws' favorite guy until Teddy came along. Think about it! How would you feel if your daughter decided to marry an older guy who was divorced, had a son, and made his living as a pro wrestler? Thank the Lord for Teddy, who warmed up Mel's parents—even toward me!

The face of wrestling was rapidly changing, thanks most specifically to the World Wrestling Federation under the capable direction of Vince McMahon. He began cleaning up the image of wrestling by making several key changes:

making it less violent

taking away the blood and gore

introducing wilder, more cartoonlike characters

dressing the wrestlers in brightly colored Spandex outfits

generally making it a sport more suitable for our most loyal demographic group in the audience: kids

Like most other non-WWF wrestlers, I initially felt that Vince was destroying wrestling with his ideas. To me, it appeared to reduce the sport to a more slapstick form. But all of us had to admit that Vince was a marketing genius. It wasn't long before the World Wrestling Federation was the hottest ticket in town. In March of 1985, Vince promoted an event called "Wrestlemania I." It was a phenomenal success, leading to "Wrestlemania II" the following March.

The WWF was on a roll. The question was, how would that affect the rest of us?

WORKING IN JAPAN

Initially, business was pretty good in the Mid South region as well. I was in an especially good spot, because I was also enjoying a big break that I received from my friends in Japan. I became a tag-team partner with Stan Hansen, who was without a doubt the biggest name in wrestling in Asia. We had a great time together, because Stan and I had a lot in common. Not the least of which was that he, too, was a former student at West Texas State University. It was fun, exciting, and quite lucrative for me to be touring Japan.

The Mid South region, in an attempt to keep up with the new standards set by the WWF, changed its name to the Universal Wrestling Federation, or the UWF. But it appeared to be too little, too late. Vince McMahon's success was good for the wrestling business but murder on the smaller, regional groups. One by one, they started to fall by the wayside.

In March of 1987, as I was preparing to go on one of my trips to Japan, a buddy of mine named Bruce Pritchard mentioned to me that he was going up to New York to apply for a position with the WWF. "Throw my name around up there," I suggested to him, half-kidding but half-serious. "Let's just see if there is any interest."

Bruce said he would do that, and I was off to Tokyo.

While I was over in Japan, I picked up a newspaper one morning that told about a new attendance record being set for an indoor event. I figured it was something that had taken place over here in Japan. In amazement, I read on to see that the event had just been held at the Pontiac Silverdome, near Detroit, where 93,000 people were in attendance. And my eyes bugged out when I discovered the event everyone had come to see…Vince McMahon's "Wrestlemania III."

ON TO THE WWF?

I had thought going back to the WWF would be a good idea. Now I thought it was a *great* idea.

When I returned from Japan, I was met with some changes. I was told that Bill Watts had sold the UWF to a family named Crockett. I met with Jim Crockett, who assured me that I had a place on their payroll. Meanwhile, Bruce Pritchard was anxiously trying to reach me. "Ted," he said breathlessly, once we made contact, "the WWF is interested in you, so whatever you do, don't sign anything with the Crocketts!"

I took Bruce's advice and told Jim I would get back to him with an answer. Not too long after that, my phone rang.

"Ted?" the voice on the other end asked. "It's Vince McMahon calling."

"Hi!" I said, with a mixture of shock and joy.

"Listen, Ted, we're *very interested* in you coming to work for the WWF," he went on. "As a matter of fact, I have an idea for a new character that has never been done before."

"What kind of character?" I asked, my curiosity aroused.

"I don't want to discuss it over the phone," Vince replied with a touch of mystery in his voice. "Here's what I would suggest: How about if I fly you up here, and we'll talk about it face to face?"

"Sure, that sounds fine," I answered.

Compliments of Vince McMahon, I flew to New York City, where I was met by a stretch limousine that would take me to the headquarters of the World Wrestling Federation, located outside of the Big Apple in Stamford, Connecticut. I took one look at the building and knew the WWF was doing well. The offices were brand-new, plush, and impeccably decorated.

When I walked into Vince's office, the first thing that caught my attention was a huge photo the size of a poster hanging on the wall behind his desk. It was an aerial photo of the recent "Wrestlemania III" crowd at the Pontiac Silverdome. That shot and Vince's natural self-confidence were a winning combination in his negotiations with a young wrestler like me.

"Ted," Vince began, "like I said over the phone, I have an idea for a character that is unique. It has never been done before, and I am completely convinced that you would be perfect for it."

"OK," I replied. "I'm ready to hear all about it. What is this new character you have in mind?"

"I can't tell you," he said, to my surprise.

"You can't tell me?" I repeated.

"No. I can't tell you unless you first commit to join the WWF." He folded his hands on the desk in an end-of-discussion manner.

"Why?"

"Look at it from my perspective, Ted. If I tell you this great idea, and you decide not to work for me, you'll go off and develop it somewhere else. No, I'm not giving away a good idea."

"I see," I replied.

"So, Ted, will you sign on to work for the WWF?"

"I think I need a little time to sort this through with my wife and family," I said, my head spinning.

"I understand," Vince replied. "Go home, talk to your wife, then give me a call with your answer. Does that sound fair?"

"Yes sir," I replied.

We stood, shook hands, and shortly I was back on a plane to Mississippi. I wanted to cheer at the top of my lungs in the middle of the flight, and I was chomping at the bit to tell everyone my good fortune. I gave the news to Mel, who was both shocked and happy for what appeared to be happening.

One of the first folks I spoke with after Melanie was Terry Funk. He was like a big brother to me, as well as a mentor, and I knew he would give me wise counsel. Plus, he was so knowledgeable about the business I felt I could completely trust him. When I told him of my conversation at WWF headquarters, I asked, "So what do you think I should do, Terry?"

He looked me squarely in the eyes, grabbed me by the shoulders, and smiled broadly. "Ted, if Vince McMahon has an idea, pack your bags, go to New York City, and don't look back!"

That's all I needed to hear.

I called Jim Crockett to tell him that I was going to leave the UWF in order to take a job with the WWF. Then I called Vince McMahon.

"Vince, count me in," I said joyously.

"That's great news, Ted," he replied.

"So, now can you tell me your idea?" I prodded.

"No. I don't want to talk about it over the phone. I will put two plane tickets in the mail for you and your wife. I want you to come back to New York City as my guests!"

THE MILLION DOLLAR MAN IS BORN

A few days later, Melanie and I were off on a fantasy trip. We flew first class to New York City. The stretch limousine was again waiting to take us to the WWF headquarters in Connecticut. Once we arrived, Melanie was entertained in the outer office, while I was invited in to talk with Vince and one of his associates, Pat Patterson.

"Ted, you've made the right decision," both Vince and Pat assured me as we talked in Vince's office.

"I know I have," I agreed.

"So, are you ready to hear my idea?" Vince taunted.

"Yes sir, I am," I answered.

"OK, here it is." Leaning in toward me, he explained his concept. "I want to create a character who is so filthy rich that he throws money around like it's nothing." He began to smile as he continued, "He is the kind of guy who can buy anyone or anything. He's a character whose god is money. I see him as a man who lives by the motto, *Every man has his price.*"

By now, I was smiling. I liked where this was going.

"I see the full visual effect," Vince went on. "You will travel all over in first class. There will be a limousine at every hotel and venue to take you where you need to go. You'll always have a wad of money on you. We'll find you a man to be your personal bodyguard and valet."

"This sounds fabulous!" I exclaimed.

"Ted, you're going to be the hottest, most hated heel in all of wrestling," Vince added, his eyes sparkling.

"It sure sounds like it," I said.

"The only thing I don't have nailed down is the name," he mused, stroking his strong chin.

Without missing a beat, I piped up, "I know what we should call him. How about the *Million Dollar Man?*"

Vince and Pat both broke into broad grins. "That's it!" Vince affirmed. "The Million Dollar Man!"

"This is gonna be big!" Pat echoed.

"Well, Ted, to start it all off," Vince continued, "I want you to go off and live like this Million Dollar Man." He escorted me out of his office, then sent Melanie and me off in his limo for a few days of splendor in New York City.

We were given a gorgeous room at the Helmsley Palace in Manhattan. A gourmet dinner was next at the world-famous Water Club restaurant. Then it was two seats, orchestra-level, up-front, to see the Broadway musical *Cats*.

Throughout the trip, I kept whispering to Melanie, "Pinch me, Mel. This has to be a dream! What just happened is the start of something big!" She would smile at me, sharing my disbelief at all that was taking place.

GETTING IN CHARACTER

The next few months were filled with carefully orchestrated preparations to make the Million Dollar Man as hated as possible. All the vignettes I mentioned in the first chapter—like clearing out the public swimming pool and kicking the basketball away from the little kid—were presented one by one, week after week, in anticipation of this new heel. I was introduced to Mike Jones, a great guy who is a good friend to this day. He was hired as "Virgil," my bodyguard and valet. In keeping with my character, I could be ruthlessly mean and degrading to him as well.

The story line for the Million Dollar Man led me ever closer to the WWF Championship title. "Every man has his price, so I can buy anything," I would brag during the interviews. "I can even buy the WWF Championship title without dripping a single bead of sweat!"

My bragging was moving right along with another big event in the WWF story line. Hulk Hogan and Andre the Giant, for years friends and fellow baby faces, were in the middle of a feud that was to be settled in a match at Market Square Arena in Indianapolis. This was the first time they had met since the record-breaking Wrestlemania III.

REAPING MY REWARDS

Holding the championship belt that night was the culmination of years of hard work. As Hulk held the twin referees in his massive hands, I clutched the reward that had come from all those hot summer nights in those small town venues. It was the payoff for all those miles on dusty, two-lane highways in the middle of nowhere. The belt was the prize for all those Bologna Blowouts, all the nights on a box springs in a cheap motel, all the pain, the blood, the scars.

I had paid my dues.

12
THE WHIRLWIND

A long time ago I heard a speaker define the word *ego* as E. G. O., Edging God Out." That's a definition that has stuck with me over the years, not only because it's accurate, but also because it describes my exact behavior during my years of growth as the Million Dollar Man.

One of the saddest parts of my whole story is that all along I knew I would be better off if I submitted my life to the Lord. But I was just too stubborn. There were small portions of my life that I would try to get in order, but it wouldn't last for very long. I was having such a selfishly good time in my new lifestyle that I forgot about God.

Shortly before I joined the World Wrestling Federation as the Million Dollar Man, Melanie and I had been searching for a church home in the area of our hometown of Clinton, Mississippi. We discovered Morrison Heights Baptist Church, which is where we decided to settle.

Mel and I both enjoyed the messages we heard from the pulpit. The pastor, Dr. Ken Alford, was a real man of God. It didn't take long for him to become a man I deeply respected. We began a friendship that has grown and continues to this day.

"GET READY"

Dr. Ken isn't just a pastor to me. He's also a friend who isn't afraid to be honest with me about where my life is headed. One day, he demonstrated that honesty.

"Ted, you'd better get ready," Dr. Ken warned me after the morning service.

"Get ready for what?" I replied, a bit confused by his statement.

"There are big tests ahead for you," he answered. "So you had better get ready." It was as if the Lord had shown him that my life would be caught up in a whirlwind in the days ahead.

I'll be OK, I thought to myself, trying my best to brush Ken's words out of my mind. I didn't think I needed a warning. I had paid my dues. It was time to really enjoy life!

But Dr. Ken was right. I should have been preparing for what was about to occur. I was not ready for the new lifestyle that was provided by the creation of the Million Dollar Man. I got caught up in it in a big way. As I had in my college days, I forgot about the Lord as my ego came on strong.

March of 1988 was a big month in my world, both personally and professionally. On the home front, Melanie gave birth to another little baby boy, whom we named Brett. In spite of my rebellion, our family was growing, and the Lord was blessing us with healthy, happy children.

Pro Wrestling on the Rise—and I Rise with It

Much of the growth of professional wrestling can be charted by observing its annual premiere event, Wrestlemania, which provides a good map of my own career as well. My first Wrestlemania event after I bought the championship belt from Andre was Wrestlemania IV, in March of 1988. The site for the event was the Atlantic City Convention Center in Atlantic City, New Jersey, home of the Miss America Pageant. Because we were in that city, there was a Donald Trump connection. We were staying at one of his luxury hotels, and he was in attendance, sitting in the front row with his then-wife, Ivana.

The main event that night was billed as a tournament to crown a new champion. Randy Savage and I ended up wrestling to determine who would be the undisputed king of professional wrestling.

I was pumped up for the match, and it initially went my way once we got started. I was working Randy over pretty well. But I was in for a surprise.

Out of the darkness beyond the ring came a man still angry at losing the belt six months earlier. Hulk Hogan exploded into the ring, smashing me with a metal folding chair. It was two against one, as Randy took advantage of Hulk's help. Before I knew it, the match was over, and Randy was declared the new champion. The crowd went wild, loving every minute of hating the Million Dollar Man! (Although I lost the title to Savage that night, I was undaunted in my quest for a title. I created a new belt—the Million Dollar Belt—as a title for myself. The belt, made of hundreds of diamonds in the shape of three large dollar signs, became one more symbol of how I could buy anything.)

Wallowing in Big Bucks

After the match, Donald and Ivana Trump made their way backstage to meet some of us and to congratulate us on the entertaining show. "Where's the

Million Dollar Man?" he asked above the roar of the backstage crowd, craning his neck from side to side.

"I'm over here," I answered, waving my hand.

"Great! Where's a photographer?" he said, looking around the whole area. "I want my picture taken with the Million Dollar Man!"

We all laughed and made sure he was granted his request. Two wealthy financial tycoons, together at last!

The wrestling magazines had a great time linking the great wealth of Donald Trump with the story line of the Million Dollar Man. Even a few years later, when Trump was having his financial troubles, the magazines would draw analogies like this one that appeared in 1990:

> Newspaper reports printed in mid-August show that businessman Donald Trump would, if he quickly sold off all his assets today, be in debt to the tune of $300 million.
>
> The $300 million figure is based on a worst-case scenario, in which properties such as his massive Mar-a-Lago estate in Florida, his Atlantic City casinos, and his Trump Tower condominium would be sold off quickly in a soft real estate market.
>
> In a best-case scenario, in which real estate values would be higher and sales wouldn't have to be made so quickly, Trump might in fact remain on the plus side in the amount of roughly $700 million. How many bills could DiBiase cover if he sold off the million dollar belt and his other assets? Perhaps he ought to start calculating.

Wrestlemania IV was so successful in Atlantic City that the decision was made to return there for Wrestlemania V. In 1989, Hulk Hogan would regain the championship title.

THE BIG BUSINESS OF PRO WRESTLING

The World Wrestling Federation was on such an amazing roll at this time that the rest of the business world was staring in disbelief. In a major way, the WWF was putting pay-per-view on the map. Some of the business schools were using us as case studies for successful marketing strategies.

By 1989, we were marketing a wide variety of wrestling-related toys and games. The WWF video arcade game was launched, as well as a home version of the video game for the Nintendo Company. This led to the release of action figures of the major wrestlers, like Hulk, Jake the Snake, the Ultimate Warrior, Randy Savage, and, of course, the Million Dollar Man.

The Tonka Toy Company then introduced a first for its toy line. Known best for producing the metal trucks we all grew up playing with, Tonka jumped from "hard" to "soft" toys by making major wrestling characters of the WWF into soft, stuffed dolls about eighteen inches tall. Called "Wrestling Buddies" by Tonka, they were a huge seller. (My youngest son, Brett, grew up with a Wrestling Buddy of his dad, which he fondly called his "Daddy Doll." Melanie and I still laugh about the time when Brett first realized that all little kids don't have a doll of their fathers. He was genuinely sad and confused!)

WWF: Going International

In 1990, Wrestlemania VI was held at the Skydome in Toronto, Canada. Once again, a new record was set for attendance. Robert Goulet was invited to begin the event with the singing of the Canadian national anthem. I was on the card, wrestling Jake the Snake Roberts. Mary Tyler Moore was seated ringside, cheering us on. In the match for the title, Hulk surrendered his championship belt, this time to the Ultimate Warrior.

It was appropriate that Wrestlemania VI was outside of the United States, for 1990 was the year of big international expansion for the WWF. We had a huge event in Tokyo, Japan, where I wrestled the Ultimate Warrior, to the delight of thousands of screaming fans. From there we went to the island of Guam. Later that same year we wrestled in England, Ireland, Germany, and Spain, as we opened up the European market.

Those were great days for the WWF, and I was enjoying the ride!

The Evil of the Million Dollar Man

By 1991, it was time for the Million Dollar Man to sink to his most evil roots. It was time to turn against my best friend. Since the creation of my character several years before, my constant sidekick had been my bodyguard, Virgil. Wrestlemania VII, held in the Sports Arena in Los Angeles, featured a match where I took on Virgil. Everyone hated the Million Dollar Man, and I loved every minute of it! Rowdy Roddy Piper was in Virgil's corner, adding to the drama of the match. I was an equal opportunity employer in that I would abuse anybody!

By the end of that year, I ventured into the world of tag-team wrestling. A championship-caliber team was created, featuring myself and Irwin R. Shyster, or I.R.S. Calling ourselves "Money, Inc." we were unbeatable. We became the tag-team champions in short order. (In real life, Irwin R. Shyster is my good buddy, Mike Rotunda. A former tight end at Syracuse University, Mike is a wonderful family man and a good friend. Today's wrestling fans may know him as Michael Wallstreet, now of the New World Order.)

Wrestlemania VIII took place in March of 1992 in the Hoosier Dome in Indianapolis. I.R.S. and I successfully defended our tag-team belts in an exciting match.

ON TOP, BUT IN A LOSING BATTLE

I was on the top of the heap in professional wrestling. It was a great time for my career, but I was fighting a battle in my personal life that I was losing. I was becoming more and more like the character of the Million Dollar Man. I wasn't mistreating people like the character did, but I was getting caught up in the celebrity status I had been enjoying. There was a seductive glamour about appearing as a guest on *Lifestyles of the Rich and Famous* with Robin Leach. It was alluring to be on the *Arsenio Hall Show*. I got caught up in the glitz of chatting with Regis and Kathie Lee.

I was having a good time, completely forgetting the warning I had brushed off from Dr. Ken. Melanie was trying to be as patient and understanding as possible, but I saw the stress and strain affecting our relationship.

I was in my own world, feeling that I needed no one else, not even God.

My self-sufficiency probably had a lot to do with the way my father raised me. I can still recall an incident between my father and me that demonstrated his kind of self-sufficiency. I had just become a teenager back in Omaha, Nebraska, and it was the dead of winter, a brutal time in the Midwest. The town fathers would come outdoors after the first storm and bank off a section of the park we lived by. Then they would flood it so we could use it as an ice skating rink.

My friends and I would choose up sides for a rousing game of ice hockey. Because I was so much bigger than everyone else, I was usually drafted to play goalie. On this particular occasion I was playing goalie without any protection to speak of. I had a baseball glove, a catcher's chest protector and a goalie's stick, and that was it. I had no mask, no knee pads or shin guards, or anything else.

As you can imagine, I had to be at the top of my goalie game or risk possible injury. One day the opposing team took a shot that looked pretty routine to everyone, including me. It was a higher shot than most, so I lifted my head, positioning my glove for the catch. Unfortunately, as I raised my head, I lost the puck in the bright winter sunlight. The next time I saw the puck, it was an inch away from my face. It hit me full force, squarely on the nose. The blow sent me sprawling to the ice, blood flowing everywhere.

My friends panicked. "Go get his dad!" they shouted to one another in their confusion.

Dad was summoned, and he came immediately. I remember how he carefully wiped the blood out of my eyes, now filled with tears.

"Can you see?" he asked in his concern.

"Yes sir, I can see," I responded.

"Should we take him to see a doctor, Mr. DiBiase?" one of my friends asked politely.

"That's a good idea," Dad replied.

"Let's carry him over to the car," the friend suggested, taking pity on my bloody condition.

"Just a minute," Dad interrupted. Turning his attention back to me, he said, "Teddy, is there anything wrong with your legs?"

"No sir," I answered honestly.

"Fine," Dad continued. "Do you know what I want you to do?"

"No," I said, shaking my head.

"Get up and walk!"

My friends looked at one another in shocked disbelief. They were all angry at my father. They all felt sorry for me, and here was my dad trying to toughen me up! My friends thought a broken nose and the need for stitches would make me weak. But my father thought it should make me strong. As always, in a battle between Dad and my friends, Dad won.

I walked to the car. Actually, I recall walking to the car with a degree of pride. *I can handle anything all by myself,* I remember thinking. Dad was trying to teach me a positive lesson.

My dad taught me much about personal pride. He instilled in me the concept that I was strong enough to pick myself up, no matter what. Of course, he never intended for me to conclude that I didn't need God. If it's possible to be grieved in heaven, I'm sure Dad must have felt that way during these wayward years of mine. I forsook the number-one priority of my dad's life, which was to honor the Lord.

I hadn't been honoring the Lord, and if things didn't change, I was going to destroy myself and my family. Little did I know at the time that things were about to change in a swift and dramatic way. I was on my way toward hitting bottom.

13
HITTING BOTTOM AND FINDING FORGIVENESS

It had to come crashing down eventually.

As the Million Dollar Man, I was making more money than I ever imagined possible in the world of wrestling. And Vince McMahon stayed true to his word. He kept up the first-class treatment everywhere I went.

But in the midst of this whirlwind, something terrible slowly and subtly took place in my life. The Million Dollar Man became less of an act for the public and more of the real me. I began to yield to some of the temptations that were coming my way as a result of my celebrity status.

The jump from the *el cheapo* budget motels to the four-star luxury hotels had an influence on me. It became commonplace to wake up in a first-class suite, order a room-service breakfast, and sign a bill for more than $30 for the meal alone (which was about the same rate I used to pay for the entire room at a cheap motel!).

To put it another way, I became worldly. The most important person in my life was *me*. Where the focus of my life should have been on God, my wife, and my kids, I increasingly became caught up in myself.

I've arrived, I thought to myself proudly. *I've worked for twelve years paying my dues in order to reach the status I'm currently enjoying*, I continued to rationalize. I was basking in my own glory, and I was losing touch with reality. It was all about ego. I was "Edging God Out" in my life. But God, as He will do with those He loves, decided to get my attention.

CAUGHT RED-HANDED!

After Wrestlemania VIII concluded in the spring of 1992, I hopped a plane out of Indianapolis to Chicago. I was scheduled for a brief layover in the Windy City before departing for London for the beginning of a European tour. Once I was settled in my hotel, I phoned Melanie back in Mississippi.

The conversation was far from chitchat or small talk. Melanie had become aware of some of the situations in which I had become involved that just weren't right. There's really no value in giving specifics here, but suffice it to say that I was not living a holy life. Melanie decided that the best way to handle it was to confront me directly.

I swallowed hard, knowing the only thing to do was to admit to my wrongdoing, which I did. It was one of the most difficult conversations I have ever had in my entire life, knowing that on the other end of the phone line was the woman who meant everything to me, but who was suffering such intense pain because of my actions.

"I'm sorry, Mel," I whispered. "I'll cancel my trip to Europe. I'll come home on the next plane out of here."

"No, don't do that," Melanie insisted. "I'm so mad at you right now, I don't *want* you to come home."

"But, Mel…" I pleaded.

"Just go on to Europe," she concluded, and she hung up the phone, ending our conversation.

I sat in the quietness of the empty hotel room, and the silence overwhelmed me. Facing up to Mel was forcing me to face up to myself. "What am I going to do now?" I cried, slamming my fist down on the nightstand. "Who can I turn to? Who can help me make sense out of all this mess?"

The answer flooded my mind…Hal Santos.

HELP ME!

Pastor Hal Santos had been a friend of mine since we had first met many years ago, back in Baton Rouge. All the time we had known one another, he tracked me and consistently demonstrated a genuine concern for my spiritual welfare.

As I sat in that hotel room, desperate for some answers, I knew that if anyone could help me, it would be Hal. Paging through my address book, my hands shaking nervously, I found the page with Hal's telephone number and placed the call to his home in Belleville, Illinois.

"Hal? It's Ted DiBiase."

"Ted! It's great to hear your voice," Hal began. "Are you at home or on the road?"

"I'm in Chicago, Hal…and it's not going very well. I'm at the end of my rope. I really need some help."

"What's wrong?" Hal inquired gently.

"I've been selfish and stupid," is the answer I gave him.

"I see," he replied.

"Hal, can you come up here? Can you fly up here and spend some time with me, please?"

Hal said he had to check on a few things, but he promised to call me back right away. I paced my hotel room like a caged Bengal tiger as I waited for the call from Hal. In a matter of minutes, the phone rang.

"I'll be on the next flight," came his answer, and it was an answer I was desperately hoping to hear. We discussed the arrangements for his trip from St. Louis to Chicago. Before he hung up, he made one last observation that stayed with me for hours: "You know, Ted, you called me, but you were really crying out to the Lord."

I placed the receiver back on its cradle, knowing that Hal was insightful enough to read me like a book.

GOD'S WAKE-UP CALL

Several hours later, Hal arrived and we sat down together. I poured out my life to him, holding nothing back. We talked together, cried together, and prayed together. "God has warned you and warned you and warned you," Hal reminded me lovingly yet forcefully.

I could only nod my head, overcome with shame and the need for forgiveness.

"This is God's wake-up call for you, Ted," he said. The more we talked and prayed, the more I pleaded with God to give me one more chance to make things right, especially with Melanie.

Hal and I parted, and he flew home to Belleville. Reluctantly, I left for London, my only comfort resting in Hal's assurance that he would call Melanie to see if there was anything he could do to help us patch things up.

I had been in Europe three days when Hal called with good news.

"Ted, I've had quite a few conversations with Melanie over the last few days. Here's where it stands: If you can get back here, Melanie has agreed to meet you at my place. Can you fly to St. Louis right away?"

I contacted the tour's promoter, explaining that I had a family emergency, and he excused me from the rest of the tour. The next plane back had me on it. Once the jet touched down in St. Louis, Hal was at the gate waiting for me. We walked quietly from the baggage claim area to his car. The drive from St. Louis to Belleville is not an especially long one, but time had become surreal at that moment. I felt I was on the longest ride of my life.

Finally I broke the silence. "Hal, what am I going to tell Melanie?" I couldn't even look at him, so I just stared blankly at the highway ahead. As long as I live, I'll never forget his reply.

He turned to me and said kindly, "Ted, just remember this one thing: *The truth will set you free.*"

"So you're saying I should just tell Mel the truth?"

"Yes. I'm not promising you it'll save your marriage, but you and I both know it's the right thing to do."

COMING CLEAN

We pulled into the driveway of Hal's home, and as I got out of the car, my knees buckled and then started shaking uncontrollably. I felt like a little wimp…a baby…a failure. I greeted Melanie, sat down on the couch, took a deep breath, and told her the truth. I looked at the pain in Melanie's face, and I turned to look at Hal for support.

Reflecting on this moment, I am certain that God had His hand over the entire adventure. It was a miracle in itself that Hal was so available. To begin with, he was the pastor of a local church, with all the demands of shepherding a congregation. Added to that responsibility was his role as the chaplain for the Belleville police force.

When I first called Hal from Chicago, he said his next few days were filled with appointments. But one by one, they began to cancel. Even a scheduled visit from his in-laws was abruptly postponed, not by Hal, but by them! Time was continually being made available through amazing, out-of-the-ordinary circumstances. Coincidence? No way!

There was only one appointment that wasn't canceled. Hal and his wife were scheduled to leave the next day to take a busload of teenagers up to Chicago to attend a youth convention. The Ascension Convention was being held at the Hyatt Regency near O'Hare Airport.

After my time of confession to Melanie in the Santos's living room, we all grabbed a few hours of sleep, and the following morning the four of us adults sleepily climbed aboard a bus filled with kids. I had no idea what was in store for me at the other end of the journey.

THE ASCENSION CONVENTION

Once we arrived at the hotel and settled in, we went down to the first session, which was being held in one of the large meeting rooms on the ground floor. Hal and his wife sat with Melanie and me on the very front row of chairs. In a matter of seconds, the word had spread that the Million Dollar Man was there. But for the first time in a very long time, the notoriety didn't matter to me.

The preacher stood at the front and began his message. I must admit, I don't even remember the man's name, but his words bored a hole through me like a laser beam from God. The message God used to drill through my hardened heart was one of forgiveness. It became the only thing that was important to me as I listened to this servant of God pour out his heart. "Accept Christ as your Savior and your sins will be forgiven," was the gospel message in its simplest form.

It was all making sense to me. This is why my personal life was crashing down around me. It was like Hal said, God had tried over and over to get my attention. Now I was at a place where I was listening.

As the sermon concluded, the preacher gave an altar call. He invited those who wanted to receive this forgiveness to get up out of their seats and to come to the front of the room. It was the most significant time in my life. Normally, I would never want anyone to see any trace of emotion from me, but tonight was not a normal night. Once he explained the altar call, I was the first person to respond. Immediately, I stood to my feet and walked forward.

Finally, I ended up at the foot of the Cross. For years I had professed Christ, but I had selfishly held on to ego. That night in Chicago was the night it all became real. I was born into the family of God!

I knelt down, offering up this prayer to the Lord: "Dear God, forgive me for being so selfish. I want You to come into my life and take full control. I'm not holding back like I've done before. This time I want You to be the Captain of my ship. I'm just along for the ride."

No sooner had I finished praying than I began to feel hands placed on both of my shoulders, on my arms, and on my hands. The front of the room became filled with teenagers, accepting Christ in their own lives and surrounding me in a show of support. Without saying a word, they were telling me they would hold me up in prayer!

The strong he-man, the Million Dollar Man, Ted DiBiase broke down and wept uncontrollably in front of all those kids that night. As I cried buckets of tears, Hal's words kept coming back into my mind—*The truth will set you free.*

I knew then that in order to make my life right with the Lord, I needed to have the faith to trust Him then and there. I knew that if I did that, He would cause everything in my life to fall into its proper place.

FORGIVE ME, MELANIE?

I looked back through the crowd of teenagers to try to observe Melanie's response to what was happening. I got up off my knees and headed back to my seat. As I approached her, I knew what she must be feeling. Understandably, I had hurt her deeply with my selfish life. She wanted with all her heart to believe what was taking place was real. I knew my assignment: I would have to prove myself to her over the test of time. And I was willing to do that if she was willing to hang in there with me.

She told me she was willing to stay with me, and to this day I am eternally grateful that the Lord has given me such a wonderful woman. Through God's grace, she was surrounded by strong Christian girlfriends who supported her through this ordeal. Instead of telling her to divorce me and take me for all the money I was worth, they told her, "Confront him, Melanie. Hear him out. See if you can discern in your own heart whether he's genuinely sorry for what he did, or if he's just sorry for getting caught." They added, "If he's truly sorry and if he's willing to change his life, the Lord says you should forgive him."

And that's what she did.

ANYTHING TO SAY?

The next event on the schedule that evening was a time slot for workshop sessions, known as break-outs. Hal was scheduled to speak at one of these break-outs, so the three of us tagged along with him; we had no idea what else to attend. As we walked into a much smaller room in another part of the hotel, Hal turned to me and asked me a question that caught me off guard: "Ted, is there anything you want to say to these kids?"

"Me?" I asked. I looked at him more closely, thinking he had to be joking.

"Yes, Ted. You." He was perfectly serious.

"Well...OK," I responded, not even knowing what I could possibly say after what had taken place at the altar.

What I did say came from a man who had known real brokenness. From the depths of my heart I spoke to the small group of wide-eyed, receptive teenagers: "You see before you a man who is supposed to have it all," I began, the words starting to choke up in my throat. "But I am here tonight to tell you that without Christ in my life I have *nothing.*"

I didn't have a lot more to say, so I thanked them for listening to me, found my seat, and listened to Hal make his presentation. My mind was blurry with all that was taking place.

TOUCHING THE LIVES OF OTHERS

When the session was over, a man approached me and said, "Excuse me, sir, but may I have a minute of your time?" He was so kind in his demeanor that I immediately consented. We moved over to a quiet corner of the meeting room where we could hear one another.

"I am a minister," he said, as he introduced himself to me. "I feel that I have to tell you something." He paused as if what he was about to say was very difficult for him. "I don't mean to sound cold or hard, but the truth is that I am seldom brought to tears by the words of another person."

I nodded to assure him I understood what he was saying and to invite him to continue. Once again, he paused for a brief moment, as if he needed to catch his breath.

"Sir," he finally spoke again in subdued tones, "you brought me to tears by what you said to those teenagers. God has used you tonight, young man." Spontaneously we reached out and embraced, holding on to each other for quite some time, and the tears once again flowed freely. I've thought back many times and for many reasons to that evening in Chicago. I've thought about how God used that evening, not only to bring me to Himself, but to launch me toward a ministry specifically geared to kids. The Lord really convicted me to reach out to those around me. In the WWF, the strongest age demographic is young people. Maybe God has allowed me to go through what I have—the good and the bad—in order to show others the value of having Christ in their lives.

THE TEST OF THE ROAD

The convention was a time of growth and healing for me. The four of us adults went back to Belleville on the bus, and Mel and I stayed a few more days at the

Santoses' home. But each day brought me closer and closer to the inevitable…soon it would be time for me to go back on the road.

This time in our lives really highlights the amazing strength of my wife. "I'm not going to be checking up on you all the time," she told me as I packed to leave on that first trip after Chicago. "I don't have to do that. You've committed yourself to the Lord, right?"

"That's right, Mel," I answered.

"So, then if you mess up, I won't have to get you," she paused, "'cause God will!"

Wise words from a wise woman.

Make no mistake about it, the life of a professional wrestler on the road is a life of constant temptation. How would I stay strong enough to avoid yielding? I knew from that moment forward that it was not going to be easy. As a kid growing up as a Roman Catholic, I had learned enough from the priests about the way the devil works in people's lives. I knew he would be operating *very subtly* in my life. I imagined his strategy for me wouldn't be to push me off a cliff, but to tempt me to gradually slide down a hill.

The Scripture passage that was given new meaning to me at this point in my life was in the Psalms. I still read this portion of the Bible almost every day, because it reminds me where I came from and where I am going:

I waited patiently for the LORD;
And He inclined to me, and heard my cry.
He brought me up out of the pit of destruction, out of the miry clay;
And He set my feet upon a rock making my footsteps firm.
And He put a new song in my mouth, a song of praise to our God;
Many will see and fear,
And will trust in the LORD.

Thou, O LORD, wilt not withhold Thy compassion from me;
Thy lovingkindness and Thy truth will continually preserve me.
For evils beyond number have surrounded me;
My iniquities have overtaken me, so that I am not able to see;
They are more numerous than the hairs of my head;
And my heart had failed me.

Be pleased, O LORD, to deliver me;
Make haste, O LORD, to help me.

(PSALM 40:1–3, 11–13, NASB)

I related so closely to the words of King David that I wondered if he had ever been out on the professional wrestling circuit.

14
BABY STEPS

The tag-team of the Million Dollar Man and Irwin R. Shyster continued its championship success for many more months. As Money, Inc., we were the WWF world tag-team champions, and no one could take our gold championship belts away from us.

We were having a great time as champions. The world of professional wrestling can be so much fun, because one never knows what's going to happen next. The competition is intense, but the friendships run deep once we are outside the ring.

As usual in this business, everything was pointing toward the next major event, Wrestlemania IX, scheduled to take place in the spring of 1993. The venue was Caesar's Palace in Las Vegas, Nevada. Money, Inc. was scheduled to wrestle a tough tag-team consisting of Brutus the Barber Beefcake and the always popular Hulk Hogan. The surrounding hype was built to an incredible high.

Deep inside of me, I had some very strong feelings at that time in my life. It was right around the time of Wrestlemania IX, but it had very little to do with wrestling. Instead, my mind was dominated by a most wonderful woman. My grandmother was just a few short breaths away from death.

TELLING GRANDMA I LOVE HER

A few months before Wrestlemania IX, I visited Grandma in the hospital, thinking it might be the last time I saw her alive. But after that visit, she rebounded and was sent home. Then once again, she took a turn for the worse and fell into a coma. I immediately flew to my brother's home in Tucson, where she had been living for the previous few years. There I stood, holding the hand of the woman who had raised me, and she couldn't hear anything I was saying to her. And I had so much I wanted to say!

Prayer was a discipline I had long forsaken, but in my newfound faith, I once again began talking with the Lord. I remember kneeling to pray fervently by Grandma's bedside: *Dear Lord, please hear my prayer. I want to be able to look my grandmother square in her eyes and tell her that I love her. Please, Lord, let it be.*

As the months passed, and our family knew my grandmother's life was nearing an end, we brought her home. I loved her so much, and I just wanted to tell her one last time. And I got that opportunity. In the Lord's wonderful grace, He saw to it that my grandmother rebounded. She briefly came out of her coma, and I had the awesome privilege to stand at her bedside and hold her hand and tell her so she could hear, "I love you." I'll never forget the look in her eyes.

Not long after that, Grandma passed away. I held her hand as she breathed her final breaths here on earth. I closed my eyes, and I could visualize her embracing the Lord Jesus. It's a moment I will carry with me forever.

Immediately after Grandma's funeral and graveside service, Melanie and I boarded a plane to Las Vegas for Wrestlemania IX. I had a very limited amount of time to move from my grief into my character as the Million Dollar Man. There's not much time for grieving in this business.

BACK TO THE GRIND

The story line that set up this title match between Money, Inc. and Hulk and Brutus was centered around the true-life crisis that Brutus the Barber Beefcake had endured. While parasailing during a day off, he crashed and fell face first, breaking all the bones in his face. The doctors patched him up, literally restructuring his face through surgery. From that point on, he always wore a mask when he wrestled.

I.R.S. and I had been attacking him verbally in response to the taunting he was sending our way. Finally, on one of the *Monday Night Raw* episodes, we physically attacked him in the ring, which set up the necessity for an old friend of Beefcake's to make a bit of a comeback in order to defend his old buddy. Hulk Hogan had actually grown up with Brutus, so this was a natural way for him to put his energies toward defeating us. The World Wrestling Federation also saw this as the perfect opportunity to bring Hogan back into a full-time position in the wrestling world.

Hulk, who was enjoying a frenzied popularity at this time, had cut back his wrestling to a part-time commitment. There were movie offers, television spots, commercials, endorsements, and a whole menagerie of people seemingly throwing money at him from every direction. But when he saw an old sidekick attacked by Money, Inc., the Hulkster was motivated to return to action.

Caesar's Palace was electric with energy that night, and the stage was set for a tag-team match with intense fan interest.

The match was filled with drama, and no one was certain who would be the victorious team. When it was all over, I.R.S. and I actually lost, but we retained the belts because we lost through disqualification. The World Wrestling Federation rules state that belts cannot be exchanged when a disqualification is involved. So, once again, we dodged a speeding bullet.

DAY-TO-DAY TESTS

The fraternity of men who crisscross the country on the professional wrestling circuit are great guys for the most part, but I quickly rediscovered what I had known all along—there aren't many Christians in professional wrestling. This is a profession filled with guys who like to be seen as tough customers. Even though they have their sensitive sides, it's not something the viewing public is allowed to see. And most of us don't show each other that side of ourselves either.

Returning to the road was going to be a real test of my newfound faith. I could only hope and pray that I would be strong enough to deal with all the pressures. Melanie was especially aware, and I remember her gently nudging me one day right before I left on a trip.

"Ted, you're so on fire for the Lord right now," she exclaimed. "I think that's just great!" However, she was quick to add, "But the newness of your faith will probably wear off soon. Then the day-to-day tests will come."

I thought and prayed about how I could best represent the Lord in front of my coworkers. I felt strongly that the right approach was to allow folks to see the difference in me, as opposed to going in with a lot of platitudes and preaching that might be difficult to live up to. So I decided *not* to pass out Bibles. It seemed like the best testimony I could offer was to purchase a few T-shirts with Christian messages printed on them and then just let my life be an example of the difference Christ could make.

The shirts ended up being a good idea; they got the message across yet didn't ostracize me from my friends. I can honestly say that none of the wrestlers outwardly ridiculed me to any serious degree. Actually, over time I picked up a nickname that was affectionately given by my friends. They started calling this big ol' wrestler "Reverend."

WALKING, STUMBLING—AND GROWING

I discovered that the trials over my faith would not come from the taunts or verbal jabs of any associates. No, my big tests were going to be all about standing up to *temptations*. Most of my friends wanted to continue with their lives the way they had been living them. And in the past, that included wanting me to join right in with them.

"Ted, we're glad you've found Jesus in your life," they would say. "But you can still be a Christian and go down to the bar in the hotel lobby for a couple of drinks. God won't send you to hell for doing that."

My insides would start churning as I listened to them talk that way. I knew they weren't saying anything incorrect, but I also knew that if I agreed to have even *one* drink, it would open up the door for even greater temptation in my already shaky life. Of course, these issues are a lot clearer now than they were back then, and I'm afraid I learned some lessons by trial and error. There were a few occasions where I agreed to visit the lobby bar, all the while trying to stay strong, only to come face to face with my own weakness.

I learned that's what baby steps are all about. I was a spiritual infant. I wasn't perfect and I certainly wasn't as strong as I had hoped I would be. I needed Christ so I could live my life through His power, and not my own. I understand that concept so much better now that I have a little spiritual maturity under my belt. The difference between back then and now is my personal growth and inner determination. They say Rome wasn't built in a day, and I now know that neither is a strong, mature Christian. It takes time.

I did some things for which I am really sorry during that time in my life. I remember my good friend Rick Flair sensing my inner turmoil as I attempted to reconcile my former life with my new one. "Don't beat yourself up, Ted," he'd tell me, flashing his winsome smile. I would nod my head in appreciation for his concern. But then he would put his arm over my shoulder and add, "Come on, let's go downstairs and have a drink. It'll cheer you up."

I looked at Rick in silence, trying desperately to figure out what God would want me to do in this situation. In this instance, I remember rationalizing, *Well, all right, I'll go downstairs to the lobby bar for just one drink. But I won't go out to a regular bar with all of them.* In that way, I felt like I was taking a stand. It was the lobby, after all, not a tavern!

But for me, it didn't work.

I fell flat on my face. I ended up getting drunk. I was angry at Rick for making the suggestion in the first place. But it didn't take long for me to realize that it wasn't Rick's fault I had fallen. It was *my* fault. Taking responsibility for my own actions was another important baby step for me. It was a step that moved me a little further down the right course.

A PLAN TO STAY STRONG

I concluded that I was going to need a plan of attack in order to stay strong on the road as I traveled. One of the key parts of my strategy was to stay in close contact with Christian brothers who could encourage me. My buddy Hal Santos was probably the biggest help at this time. He would faithfully call me every week or so, just to check on me.

"How's it going, Ted?" he'd lovingly ask.

I had one of two responses I would usually give Hal. There was the winning answer: "I'm doing all right, Hal. I got through another week without yielding to any temptation."

Or, there was the reply of a struggling baby Christian: "I'm trying the best I can, Hal, but I'm really struggling out here."

Hal would use these phone calls as a chance to teach me a little more each time about my new faith. He was like a long-distance mentor. "Ted, your life is like a glass castle," he told me one time. "Now that you're a Christian everyone is watching you, and they can see right through you. Unfortunately, they're all just waiting for you to mess up."

It was a conversation like that one that helped me on so many of my trips. I was learning that taking a stand as a Christian is not telling people that you are perfect. No, you're still a human, still a sinner. But with Christ as the focal point of your life, the key is to continually make that earnest effort toward patterning your life after Him. That's what taking a stand is all about.

LEANING ON JESUS

One of my favorite Bible passages became the apostle Paul's words to the Corinthians:

> Do you not know that those who run in a race all run, but only one receives the prize? Run in such a way that you may win. And everyone who competes in the games exercises self-control in all things. They then do it to receive a perishable wreath, but we an imperishable.

Therefore I run in such a way, as not without aim; I box in such a way, as not beating the air; but I buffet my body and make it my slave, lest possibly, after I have preached to others, I myself should be disqualified.

(1 CORINTHIANS 9:24–27, NASB)

It's all about faith, discipline, and endurance. I remember as a child hearing a priest tell me, "The Christian life is like climbing a mountain. You'll fall, you'll bang yourself up a bit, you'll scrape your knees, you'll get bruised. But the important thing to remember is to pick yourself up and keep going. Stay close to Him, Ted, for He will never fail you."

Staying close to God became another important aspect in my strategy for spiritual victory on the road. To me, staying close to the Lord means doing things like spending time in His Word, the Bible. I decided that I was going to read my Bible every day, no matter what. Even if it's only one small chapter, I tried to make it a point to pick up the Book every day so He could speak to me.

Prayer was another vital element. I read in the New Testament the phrase "*Pray continuously*," and I was completely baffled. I thought to myself, *Does this mean I have to be on my knees twenty-four hours a day? I can't do that! I have too many other responsibilities.*

But as I continued my baby steps, I came to realize that praying continuously is more about an attitude of seeking Him in everything I do. It's the constant search to discover His will. To this day, the first thing I do every morning when I roll my body out of bed and my feet hit the floor is say a prayer of thanks to the Lord for another day He has chosen to give me.

READY TO MOVE ON

The grind of pro wrestling was starting to wear me down. I had already reached the apex of my career, and I rode the crest of that wave from 1987 all the way through 1992. After Wrestlemania IX, in April of 1993, things started on a bit of a downward swing for me professionally. It seemed like the perfect time for me to take a break.

Spiritually, I couldn't get two words out of my mind. The words were straight from the Scriptures: "*Flee temptation.*" I was in an environment where I didn't see any other Christians and that presented an atmosphere of incredible temptation. Plus, I wasn't home on any Sunday, so I wasn't getting my battery recharged through weekly fellowship with believers at our local church. The more I prayed about it, the more I felt that the Lord wanted me to get away from the WWF.

About a month after Wrestlemania IX, I decided it was time to act on what I knew to be the right direction for me. With all the courage I could muster, I walked into Vince McMahon's office and gave him notice that I was planning to leave the organization. Vince had been extremely supportive of me throughout my professional career, so this was not an easy conversation to have.

"Vince, there's something I have to do, and I am hoping that you'll understand what this is all about," I began.

"What's on your mind, Ted?" Vince inquired, sensing this was to be a pretty serious conversation.

"I'm giving you my notice," I stammered out. "It has nothing to do with being unhappy with the World Wrestling Federation or the way you are treating me. I love it here."

Vince leaned over the desk. "So what's it all about?"

"It's really all about one thing," I replied.

"What is it?"

"I just need to be able to spend more time at home with my family," I gushed out.

"I see," he commented quietly.

Pressing on, I added, "I'm just at a place in my personal life and my life with Melanie that I feel like this is the right thing to do."

Vince was quiet for a moment, then he added a comment that I had heard him make before. "Well, Ted, whatever you have to do, then you better do it."

I nodded.

"This doesn't sound like a decision that I will be able to talk you out of," he added, checking my facial expression to see if there might be the slightest hint of an opening in the door.

"No, Vince. I'm pretty firm on this one."

And with that, Vince accepted my decision, reached out to shake my hand, and wished me the best of luck. I'm sure there was a lot about my decision that he didn't understand, but we nonetheless agreed to have me stay on through the summer of 1993. His support meant a great deal to me.

My final match was in August, at Summer Slam '93 in Detroit, Michigan. It was a single match against a wrestler known back then as Razor Ramon.

(Now, as a part of the WCW, wrestling fans know him as Scott Hall, one of my buddies in the New World Order.)

He won the match, and it turned him from his previous role as a bad guy into a good guy. Once again, I was used to launch someone else into a superstar career!

Plenty of emotion welled up inside of me that hot summer evening. The World Wrestling Federation had been good to me, and it was certainly with mixed feelings that I walked away from the ring as the crowd cheered for their new man, Razor Ramon. But at the time, I had no idea how significant this match would become in my life's story.

It was the last time I would wrestle in the United States...forever.

15
FROM RING TO RINGSIDE

One of the big names in wrestling promotion in Japan is a wonderful gentleman who goes by the name of Giant Baba. When I left the World Wrestling Federation in August of 1993, I was going into a contract I had signed with Baba's organization, All Japan Pro Wrestling. I was to wrestle over there for two-week tours, followed by two weeks off back in the States. The "two weeks on, two weeks off" arrangement was to begin immediately in September.

I felt good about this agreement, because it gave me two-week periods at home with the family. Plus, it took me out of the environment of the United States wrestling circuit that provided so many temptations.

The first two weeks in September went really well. I was teamed up with my old friend Stan Hansen, Japan's hottest wrestler. Our tag-team matches were very popular all over Japan. I was pleased that the Lord seemed to be blessing my decision to flee the temptation of the World Wrestling Federation and yet continue my career overseas.

But God had a different plan.

MY BODY'S WARNING SHOT

During my two weeks of wrestling in October, I began to notice some physical symptoms that I had not felt before. There was a bolt of pain that would shoot down my arms, starting at my neck and traveling to my hands. There was numbness in my hands as well. Usually, I would just deal with it privately, being the macho guy who would just suck it up and perform through the pain. But this felt pretty serious, so when I returned home, I decided to have a doctor take a look.

The doctor's report was unsettling.

"Ted, we've run an MRI on you, and we discovered that you have a herniated disk between the fifth and sixth vertebrae of your neck," the doctor pronounced matter-of-factly.

"My neck?" I swallowed hard.

"Yes, I am afraid so," he replied.

"What can be done?" I asked.

"Basically, there are two strategies from which you can choose. The first is for you to rest. By that, I mean no more physical activity for a while so the neck can heal itself."

"Will that work?"

"It should," he replied. "But if you were to receive any sort of jarring or jolt to that part of your neck, there's no telling what would happen. Since it is herniated pretty badly, it will be a point of weakness for the rest of your life."

"Could I be paralyzed?" I asked, not sure I really wanted to hear his professional opinion.

"Yes. If it were aggravated in a certain manner, that is a definite possibility," he said soberly.

I just sat and stared at the sterile white walls that surrounded us. This was not the way it was suppose to work. *Why is this happening now, Lord?* I thought.

"OK," I said, trying to collect my senses. "You said there were a couple of options. Rest is the first one. What is my other option?"

"The other option would be for us to perform surgery on your neck," the doctor answered.

"Will that remedy the situation?"

"It will help, but you will still be facing the same risk if the neck were ever jolted or jarred."

"So what are you saying, Doc?" I blurted out.

He paused, took a long breath, and softly said, "Ted, I guess what I am saying is that, in my professional opinion, you should retire from wrestling. There's just too much risk."

I left the doctor's office in a daze. Why was this happening? How was this part of God's plan for me? What about the contract I signed with Giant Baba? Isn't it important for a Christian to honor his contracts? Isn't that part of integrity? But what if I got seriously hurt?

All of these questions went unanswered in the days immediately following my visit to the doctor. The one thing I did feel strongly about, though, was honoring my commitment to Giant Baba.

KEEPING MY WORD

I returned to Japan in the beginning of November for the start of my two-week tour for that month. It was billed as "The Tag-Team Tour," with Stan and me as the headliners. I prayed for the Lord to protect me, because I knew I couldn't let my boss and my teammates down.

I had only been in Japan three days when I felt a sharp pain speed down my arms from the base of my neck. I had been jolted in a fairly routine wrestling maneuver. I hadn't done any further damage, we would find out later, but I took it as a warning sign from above.

The risk was too great. I had to get out of wrestling.

With great disappointment and sadness, I told Giant Baba of my injury and of the doctor's prognosis. "I'm so very sorry," I apologized, "but I just can't go on with the tour."

Giant Baba was incredibly understanding. He sent me home right away, and even though I had only wrestled three days, he compensated me as if I had wrestled for the entire tour.

Looking out over the Pacific Ocean as I flew thirty-three thousand feet above it on my way home, I wondered what was going to happen next. I couldn't imagine my life without professional wrestling.

LEAVING THE RING—FOR GOOD

"Melanie, I'm done," I announced upon my early arrival home.

"What do you mean?" she asked.

"It's over. I'm out of the ring forever. Tomorrow I am going to file for my disability insurance."

She nodded in understanding. There weren't many words that could help put all this together at that point.

Fortunately for me, God gave me a wise wife. Only a year before my neck injury, I had taken out an insurance policy to cover just such a situation. She had patiently asked me to do this for years, but I was always putting it off. Thank the Lord I finally heard what she was saying.

That insurance policy was the answer for at least one of the questions that ran through my mind: How was I going to support my family if I couldn't wrestle? The settlement for a neck injury was enough to keep us financially secure for an extended period of time. Thanks to the love and foresight of my wife, we were going to be OK on that front.

BACK HOME

The end of November of 1993 was a time of reflection for me. I didn't know why things were going the way they were, but I was determined to get on with my life the best way I knew how.

In that stretch of days between Thanksgiving and Christmas, a particular time stands out in my memory. On one hand, it was a very ordinary type of situation; yet on the other hand, it was profound.

My son Teddy had been asking me to go deer hunting with him. He had fallen in love with the sport and did a lot of hunting with his grandfather, Melanie's dad. Now, with lots of extra time on my hands, I had no reason to refuse his request. Off we went early one morning to climb into a deer stand and wait for a deer.

That's when it happened for me. Sitting there with my son in the quiet countryside in the early morning hours before sunrise, I could hear every sound for miles. The winter air was crisp and cold, making me glad I had brought along some coffee and had worn plenty of sweatshirts underneath my camouflage hunting jacket. As I looked upward, the sky was crystal clear in its darkness. Every star was shining brightly, patiently awaiting the dawn.

I was overcome with a feeling of great peace. *My prayer has been answered,* I thought to myself as I sat in the cold deer stand. *I am back home. I am off the road. I am out of the tempting atmosphere of professional wrestling. And, most of all, I am spending more time with my family!*

My thoughts became overwhelming, and I began to quietly cry. As the tears rolled down my cheeks, I prayed, "Thank You, dear Lord, for allowing this injury to occur. Through it, You have answered my prayers." It was like an epiphany for me. Once again, things were right.

I huddled closer to my son, and together we watched a fabulous sunrise over the Mississippi horizon.

A NEW CAREER

In January of 1994, I went out to Los Angeles to explore another facet of my career. All my adult life, people had told me they thought my speaking voice was exceptional. The deep, bass sound I generate was always perfect for my character as a villain, but perhaps there were other ways I could use it to my advantage. I met some people who wanted me to come to the West Coast to check out the world of "voice-overs." Being the voice of a commercial or a cartoon character sounded like fun, so I went with some high expectations.

I ended up staying in Los Angeles a month, taking part in a variety of activities. I went to regular sessions with a voice-over coach. I also trained with Francois Petite, a martial-arts expert, who helped me a great deal with my physical condition. I dropped twenty unnecessary pounds that month as well. On top of all that, I was there for the Northridge earthquake that rocked southern California on January 17, 1994. (In God's great timing, He gave me my own personal earthquake the next day. On January 18, 1994, I turned forty.)

BACK TO WRESTLING?

I was content with my new life, and I worked hard that month in Los Angeles, thinking voice-over work might be my next vocation. Sometimes, though, things come our way when we aren't even looking for them. For example, a telephone call came at that very time that caught me completely off guard:

"Ted, it's Vince McMahon."

"Hi, Vince," I replied, a bit stunned.

We small-talked for a couple of minutes, and then he said, "I have a business proposition for you."

"What is it?" I asked. I had no idea where he might be headed with this conversation.

"Would you consider being a commentator for a pay-per-view event we'll be having the end of this month up in Providence, Rhode Island? We'll take good care of you."

"OK. Sure. Sounds like fun," I answered.

So a few short days later, I made my debut as a color commentator, at the Royal Rumble. I had a great time doing it too. It all came naturally to me, after having been around that world for so much of my life.

Not only did I like it, but, more importantly, the WWF liked what they saw and heard. "Ted, how about coming on board in the dual role of color commentator and ringside manager?" Vince asked.

The more I heard, the more I liked. Television work would average out to a little more than one day a week! I could still have the valuable time at home that I wanted with my family. Besides, I was more comfortable facing the tempting world of wrestling in smaller bites. I could stay strong a little at a time.

One question needed to be answered though: Would my insurance company perceive this as a return to wrestling, which would void my settlement with them? I checked with them over the phone to make sure there was no conflict with the terms of my agreement. All was clear from their point of view. Now I could put the insurance money away in savings, which was a great opportunity. And I was home!

What a wonderful answer to prayer!

I enjoyed the new challenge of becoming a commentator. I had to adjust to not being in the ring, which was the place for the spotlight, but it wasn't the major issue it could have been.

Did I miss being in the ring? I was pleased to discover my honest answer was, "For the most part, no, not really."

I was certain I didn't miss the physical abuse and the wear and tear on my weary body. It was someone else's turn to put himself through that kind of incredible demand.

To be completely honest, there were a few times when I missed being in the ring. Usually it was when a great match was taking place. I could recall the rush that overwhelmed me when I elicited the reaction from the crowd that I wanted, or how exciting it was to feel their eyes following my every move. There were some wonderful moments in my long career, and occasionally these were brought to mind through the actions of the other wrestlers. But I was content and happy just to be a part of wrestling. And I was having a great time as a commentator. I was getting good feedback too. I ended up working the most with Gorilla Monsoon, which was good fortune for me. I really respect him and all he brought to the business during his years as a wrestler and after his retirement from the ring as well.

Soon Vince wanted me to take a more active role as the manager for a stable of young athletes on their way up the ladder. Over the next few years, I was called upon to manage a wide variety of guys whose names read like a wrestling grocery list:

King Kong Bundy
Big Sid
Tatanka
Irwin R. Shyster

Stone Cold Steve Austin

In the position of manager, I was still shielded from the physical abuse, but I once again entered the world of verbal abuse. People were yelling and screaming at me all the time. But I was used to it. In fact, it reminded me of the good old days!

GROWING SPIRITUALLY

Things were going very well for me professionally, and my spiritual life was continuing to grow too. I was still in a mode of taking baby steps as a Christian toddler. But now I was more keenly aware of Satan's strategy for the downfall of Ted DiBiase. He was not holding anything back but launched a full assault on me. Thanks to a good wife and good friends like Hal Santos, I stayed accountable for my actions, which proved to make a big difference.

I learned to avoid situations where I would be the most vulnerable, including the temptations I faced on the road. Consequently, I was in continual contact with Hal by telephone.

"Remember, Ted," Hal would encourage, "it is not your strength that is going to get you through these temptations. It is only through the power of Christ that you will be victorious."

"OK, Hal," I'd reply after listening. "Just keep praying for me."

"I do, Ted. I pray for you every day."

With my new resolve and with the support I was receiving, it was a time of great spiritual awakening for me. God was teaching me a great deal, for which I was grateful. I couldn't learn it fast enough. Things were good at the WWF, the family was healthy, I was growing in my faith.

Something else was growing about this time, as well. After years of complete dominance, the World Wrestling Federation had recently developed some pretty stiff competition from a formidable foe. Ted Turner had developed his World Championship Wrestling into a national powerhouse, and the WCW was giving the WWF a real run for the number-one spot.

Ultimately, the WCW would enter my world too.

16
FROM THE WWF TO THE WCW

Monday became the night for head-on competition for professional wrestling on TV. A fan could watch the WWF on a program called *Monday Night Raw*, which ran on the USA Cable Network, or catch the WCW on a show titled *Monday Nitro*, airing on TNT.

Vince McMahon had established the World Wrestling Federation as the powerhouse in the wrestling business, and he enjoyed that favored status for many years. But the more I hung around the WWF, the more I saw guys looking over their shoulders at the WCW. The people in the WCW had committed themselves to compare with the WWF, and it was beginning to show.

Wrestlemania X took place in March of 1994, in world-famous Madison Square Garden in New York City. The WWF was continuing to pack major arenas everywhere it went, so those of us involved in that organization felt comfortable with its future. My role in Wrestlemania X was to sit in the stands directly behind a gentleman we hired to be our guest that evening. He was a dead ringer for President Bill Clinton! The camera was sure to catch many different angles of "the President," with the Million Dollar Man directly off to his right!

STILL THE MILLION DOLLAR MAN!

Even though I wasn't wrestling, I was still enjoying the notoriety that came with being the Million Dollar Man. Whether I was in an airport, at the grocery store, or on vacation with my family, I was recognized wherever I went. I've always tried to be kind to folks who want to meet me, obliging their request for an autograph or to have their picture taken with me. Now, as a Christian, when I sign an autograph, I usually add a Scripture reference as a witness underneath my name.

Some people don't know how to respond when they meet me. I still laugh when I think about one time when I walked into a men's room where there was one other guy already there. He stared at me, obviously becoming more and more excited about being in the same room with the Million Dollar Man. Finally, he couldn't contain his enthusiasm, so he walked over to me and blurted out: "Hey, man! Do you know who you are?"

Then there was the time a few years earlier when Melanie and I were with Hal Santos and his wife, Pamela, over in Hawaii. We were enjoying a quiet summer vacation on the island of Maui. One warm evening, the four of us went to a quaint little town to browse around. Hal and I found a video arcade while Melanie and Pamela were off shopping.

Hal was immediately quite amused by something, so he motioned me over to catch the action. A darling young boy was playing the WWF video arcade game, and he had chosen as his wrestler the Million Dollar Man. He was playing against a friend of his, and they appeared to be in an intense battle.

The little boy started to yell at the top of his voice: "I'm Ted DiBiase and I'm gonna smash him!"

Hal motioned to me that I should stand right behind the kid and pick the right moment to add my two cents to the match. When it looked as though he was going to beat the other kid, I bent over so that my face was directly behind this little guy. Using my best deep voice, I said to the boy, "Give him a body slam!"

Startled, the child looked around. It took a millisecond for him to recognize me. He screamed, "Oh my gosh! It's Ted DiBiase!"

Hal and I laughed till our eyes filled with tears. The wide-eyed look on that little boy's face was priceless. (By the way, we found out later that child was the son of basketball star Magic Johnson. There are wrestling fans everywhere!)

ENJOYING A NEW JOB AND NEW FRIENDS

I was having fun in my commentator position. The money was good, people were nice to me, I was home more, and I was growing in my faith. Back home in Clinton, I met a guy who would become another close friend. Our lives were in two different worlds, but the things we had in common were uncanny.

Rendy Lovelady grew up in the home of a Baptist minister. Like me, Rendy spent a period of his life wandering away from the Lord, so we had some common experiences that drew us together. At an early age, Rendy got into the music management business. Over the years he has managed acts like Van Halen and Motley Crue, to name just a couple. He reached a point just like I did, where the temptations that accompanied his business were becoming overwhelming. He returned to the Lord, and now he represents major Christian talent like Jars of Clay and the pianist Dino. (Rendy himself is a great singer!)

"You have an amazing story, Ted," Rendy commented to me.

"Yeah," I laughed. "It's a lot like yours!"

"Well, that's true," he responded. "But I think yours is a story that people ought to hear about."

"What do you mean?" I asked.

"I think you should write a book," Rendy answered. I looked to see if he was joking, but he was serious.

"Are you kidding?" I double-checked.

"No. People would be greatly encouraged by your life story. God has allowed you to go through what you have so that you can be where you are now. You've seen the good and the bad, both of which helped you realize how much you need the Lord in your life. I can relate to that, as I'm sure others will also."

"I've never thought of writing a book," I mused.

"Well, don't do it until you're ready. But I know if the time is right that God will use it."

BACK ON THE ROAD?

Wrestlemania XI was held in Hartford, Connecticut, in March of 1995. This was the famous venue where football legend Lawrence Taylor stepped into the ring to wrestle Bam-Bam Bigelow. Shortly after that event, Vince approached me about modifying my job description a bit.

"Ted, I want you to groom someone for me. Big Sid is making a comeback, and you'd be perfect as his manager," he explained.

"That would involve more time on the road, wouldn't it?" I asked, but I already knew the answer.

"A little," he replied.

"I'm not sure, Vince," I stammered.

"Think about it," he answered, patting me on the back. "I think it would be a good move."

Eventually I agreed to do it, but it wasn't what I really liked. Doing television on Monday nights, along with an occasional pay-per-view event, was the schedule that worked best for me. I had been on the road for twenty years and the thought of returning to it was pretty discouraging.

Working as a manager became my main contribution to the WWF for the next fourteen months. Granted, it wasn't the hard road that regional wrestling had been, but it was demanding nonetheless.

Good-bye WWF, Hello WCW

Wrestlemania XII, held in southern California, came and went in March of 1996. I was feeling increasingly uneasy in the WWF, partly because of the increased road time, but also because I was becoming aware of what was going on with our competition, the WCW.

One by one, some of the biggest names in the WWF were leaving to go to work for the WCW. Eric Bishoff was the man in charge of Ted Turner's organization, and he was using the Turner wealth to his advantage. Guys were being offered deals that Vince could not match. Randy Savage left, Diesel left, Razor Ramon left, Lex Lugar left. Of course, the biggest of all, Hulk Hogan, had already left the WWF in pursuit of a movie career. In the past few years he joined the WCW as well.

Because of my contract, I couldn't call anyone at WCW directly, but through the wrestling pipeline, I became aware that Eric Bishoff was thinking about hiring me. As his interest became increasingly clear, I gave my notice to the WWF in the spring of 1996.

I thanked Vince for all he had done for me. Once again, he didn't want to see me go. I tried to explain that my family was very important to me. We both knew how much he was pushing me to get out on the road even more. Once again, it was simply time for me to move on.

On Tuesday evening, May 28, 1996, I walked into the arena in Charleston, South Carolina. It was a warm night, especially humid for that early in the year. For everyone else, it was just another venue, but for me it was my final night with the WWF.

Like most nights, most of the wrestlers were backstage, huddled around TV monitors, watching the action in the ring. There is a wonderful camaraderie in this business. The guys would cheer when a good move was accomplished by one of their coworkers! (Of course, they would also groan and roll their eyes when someone attempted a bad move in the ring!)

One by one, I said farewell to the folks I had worked with for nine years. Some gave me handshakes, some gave me pats on the back, others gave me big, affectionate bear hugs. I worked my way around the entire cast of characters that made up the WWF:

Jake the Snake
the Ultimate Warrior
Shawn Michaels
Vader
Wildman Marc Mero
Ahmed Johnson
Savio Vega
the British Bulldog
Yokozuna

I also made sure to give my best to the previous generation, thanking guys like Gorilla Monsoon, Pat Patterson, and Chief Jay Strongbow for all they had taught me.

There was the typical excitement both onstage and offstage. I laughed as the British Bulldog set up an elaborate practical joke: Whoever opened the door to the men's room set off a firecracker! Meanwhile, the sellout crowd was cheering at a frenzied level.

Soon it was time for my swan song with the WWF. I walked out with my man, Stone Cold Steve Austin. In my role as his manager, I stayed ringside, pacing back and forth, cheering Steve on, taunting his opponent, Savio Vega, and distracting the referee, Earl Hebner, whenever I could.

The story line called for Savio to defeat Steve with a questionable move that caused me to go ballistic at ringside. The crowd thoroughly enjoyed my ranting and raving, which was all to no avail.

With that, I finished out my career as the Million Dollar Man. I'm not sure the local fans knew it was my last appearance, but as I left ringside and slowly sauntered down the walkway toward the backstage area, their attention was solidly focused on me. The hissing was all directed at the guy they had loved to hate for the past nine years. The taunting continued, and they started singing "Na, na, na, na. Na, na, na, na. Hey, hey, hey, Good-bye…"

That night they said their final good-bye to the Million Dollar Man. It was well after midnight when I finally left the arena. The schedule called for me to drive back to Savannah, Georgia, where that particular trip had begun. I checked into a motel in Savannah at 2:15 in the morning. I asked for a wake-up call at 5:15 so I could make my 6:30 flight back home. Three hours of sleep…a reminder of the old days.

The WWF chapter of my life ended, but I want to reiterate my love and respect for the World Wrestling Federation. Vince McMahon redefined wrestling through a marketing plan that was pure genius. He took sports entertainment, cleaned it up, dressed it up, and gave it a level of acceptance and popularity that it had never before known.

I don't want anyone to read anything negative into my leaving the WWF for the WCW. The evolution of wrestling shows that the big fish swallows the smaller fish. Just as Vince eventually put all the regional wrestling territories out of business, Ted Turner is doing the same to his competitors with the power of World Championship Wrestling. The WCW is overpowering because it is in a position to offer more compensation to the talent. This in no way discredits Vince McMahon; it just states the way it is.

Competition is healthy for our sport. The WWF is stronger because of the WCW and vice versa. We need each other to make us work as hard as we can. It's a time of strengthening for our business.

LIFE IN THE WCW—AND IN MINISTRY

My move to World Championship Wrestling was a very smooth transition for me. The ending of my time at the WWF was as amicable as it could have been, and late that summer, I glided easily into my new slot at WCW.

I was hired to be an announcer, a ringside talent, and a creative consultant. I came into the WCW not too far removed from the character I portrayed in the WWF. "The Million Dollar Man" is a character property of the WWF, so I was not able to take that character with me. But, obviously, Ted DiBiase is my real name, so nobody could change that!

As of this writing, my character is the financial backer and the cocreator of the New World Order. The NWO is an organization trying to take over the WCW. That alone should tell you that we're a group of rebels, all dressed in black.

My schedule with World Championship Wrestling once again affords me maximum time with my family. The WCW has a weekly Monday night broadcast. I work that broadcast, as well as the pay-per-views, which run approximately once a month. Even with a few personal appearances and extra TV taping days, one can see that I have a pretty light schedule.

This has opened up more availability for ministry, which is very important to me. Right after my transition from one organization to the other, I had the opportunity to appear on *The 700 Club* in November of 1996. The show's host, Pat Robertson, interviewed me about my life, career, and most importantly, my faith.

"Who is this 'Million Dollar Man?'" he asked curiously.

"I think of the Million Dollar Man as wrestling's answer to Ebenezer Scrooge," I answered. "His god was his money. He thinks he can buy anyone or anything. Every man has his price."

"Well then, tell me," Pat continued. "How did a nice Catholic boy become such a mean pro wrestler?"

With that, I was able to talk about my upbringing, my mom, and my admiration for my dad.

"But professional wrestling is such a wild world, isn't it?" Pat asked.

"Yes," I answered, "it's like a sports soap opera."

Then Pat added, "I remember we had some wrestlers who went with us one year on a tour of the Holy Land. Every now and then people recognize me and come up for an autograph or to shake my hand...but I've never seen anything like these wrestlers. They were mobbed by folks wanting autographs. You guys are incredibly popular, wouldn't you agree?"

"Yes sir."

Then the interview turned the direction I had hoped for. "But Ted, in the midst of such a violent profession, you met the Prince of Peace. You met Jesus. Tell us how that happened."

With that lead-in, I was able to tell Pat about my experience at the Ascension Convention in Chicago. I told him how I committed myself to the Lord in the middle of that room in front of several thousand teenagers.

"Kids ask me all the time, 'Ted, what was your toughest match?'"

"What's your answer?" Pat asked.

"I tell them that my toughest match was with God," I answered.

"Did God pin you?"

"No. I gave up."

It was clear that Pat was touched by the story I was telling. "Meeting Christ is the best move you ever made?" he asked.

"Yes sir," I said softly.

"No regrets?"

"None."

Pat turned to the camera. "Folks, there are those who think religion and

Jesus are only for old ladies and children. Ladies and gentlemen, you've just heard the story of a real man's man."

17
FUTURE CHALLENGES

My life has been an exciting journey, filled with high points and low points, good times and bad, and valuable lessons to be learned all along the way. But I honestly believe that the best days are ahead for the DiBiase family. God is taking care of us in a most wonderful way.

Everything that has happened to me has been for a purpose. I tried and failed, tried and failed, and tried and failed again. Yet, through it all, God has demonstrated the most incredible aspect of His character... *forgiveness.*

My favorite verse in the Bible is Philippians 4:13, which states what life is all about for me: "I can do all things through Him, who strengthens me."

I have learned to stand on that truth as the motto for my life. Whenever I fail—and I still do—as long as I lean on His strength, I will make it. When I think of all the times I have failed the Lord only to have Him forgive me, I am overwhelmed with how much He loves me. He keeps reaching out His hand to me, picking me up every time I fall. I'm falling less these days, but it's still a great comfort to know He's there.

I reached the bottom in life, yet God used my situation to open my eyes and to break me. Through my brokenness, I completely submitted myself to the Lord. It's been through that complete submission that I have learned about God's perfect peace. Before totally surrendering myself to His will, I was proudly clinging to certain areas of my life. Still holding on to my pride, I was feeding my ego, which was ultimately very unsatisfying. All my goals were caught up in my own selfish desires. I wanted to be a superstar in wrestling, which in itself is not bad, but the question was *why* did I want to become a wrestling superstar? Before I met the Lord, it was all about self-serving motives. Now I see the value in asking the all-important question: What do You want, Lord?

USE ME, GOD!

In many respects, I have no idea what's ahead for me. But I know that I want the Lord to use me in whatever way He can. God has provided such a natural platform for me to touch other people's lives. There are thousands of wrestling fans all across the world, but I'm thinking beyond that group.

I'm thinking of those people who hold up the typical stereotype of the American dream. I want to speak to those people who think rock stars, movie stars, and sports stars have it all because they have money and fame. I want those people to know that I have had all that money and fame, and it just doesn't satisfy. What does satisfy is the love of the Lord and the love of my family.

My friend and mentor, pastor Hal Santos, has been such an encouragement to me in the pursuit of my ministry. I can remember seeking his counsel immediately after I came to the Lord. His advice: Slow down!

"Hal, there are all sorts of people who are asking me to come to their church or youth meeting in order to share my testimony," I told him one day, soon after our memorable trip to Chicago.

"That doesn't surprise me," Hal replied.

"Should I agree to speak for these groups?" I pressed.

"No, not yet," he replied.

"OK," I answered, a little surprised at his response. "Do you mind if I ask you why I should say no?"

"Ted, I think the best thing for you to do is to take the next couple of years as a time for personal spiritual growth and maturity. I'm guessing that two years from now you'll be in a place of greater wisdom to share what the Lord is doing in you and through you."

As a result of Hal's wisdom, I stayed away from the speaking circuit for those crucial first two years. And Hal was right. I grew in my faith to the place that now I have much more to say about how the Lord can take a guy like me, forgive him, and make him whole.

SHARING THE FAITH

Nowadays, I speak in a wide variety of settings. I've preached in large churches, given my testimony before thousands of young people, and been a guest on *The 700 Club*. I've addressed youth camps, community and civic events, Youth for Christ functions, and even spoken at a prison.

What's especially amazing to me is that I am not really pursuing a speaking career. I'm just allowing the Lord to use me, and He is leading me to these significant opportunities.

I'll never forget one of the first times I was asked to give my testimony. The invitation came from a church in Kansas City, Missouri, asking me to speak to a group of more than one thousand young people. The first thing I did was rally my troops—I called Hal.

"Hal, can you come with me to Kansas City? They want me to give my testimony."

"I'll be there, brother," he replied.

The sponsors of the event did a great job of preparing the kids for my arrival. There was a large screen placed in the front of the auditorium, where a promotional video from the World Wrestling Federation highlighted some of the more dastardly deeds of my wrestling career. The kids were totally into the video, while I waited backstage, more nervous than I could ever remember being.

"Are you OK, Ted?" Hal kept gently inquiring.

"Sure. I'm fine. Why do you ask?"

"It's just that you keep ducking into the men's room," he replied with a wink and a chuckle.

"Keep praying, Hal," I mumbled. "Keep praying."

When the video concluded, the pastor got up to announce that the Million Dollar Man was here to talk about a part of his life that didn't appear on the video. The audience was ready. I walked to the podium on legs that felt as if they would buckle at any moment.

"The Million Dollar Man made his mark on professional wrestling by using the motto, *Every man has his price*," I began. "But I am here today to tell you that *God paid the price* when the Lord Jesus died on the Cross for our sins. If you accept Him today, He will change your life in a dramatic way. I've accepted the Lord. Listen to how He has changed my life."

From there, I launched into my testimony. The kids were sitting on the edge of their seats. The more I spoke, the more I felt God's peace. The nervousness gradually went away, and the Lord used me to minister to these great kids.

When I finished, the pastor returned to the front and asked all of us to bow our heads for a prayer of invitation. When he invited people to come forward to accept Christ as their Savior, the aisles started filling up with kids making their way to the front of the sanctuary. Not only were young people responding, but their parents came forward as well.

"This is amazing," I said to Hal after the meeting.

"God is using you, Ted," he responded.

"He sure did tonight."

"And I can tell you one of the biggest reasons why the Lord is using you," he added.

"Why?" I asked.

"Because you are telling them through your life story the value of accountability," he continued.

"Accountability?" I mused.

"Sure. Think about it," he said. "Your life would hit bottom when you got too wrapped up in your own world. But things would come together when you understood the importance of accountability on three different levels. First, you are accountable to the Lord. Second, you are accountable to your family. Third, you are accountable to an outside source—me. Through those three channels, you keep your life on track. It's a powerful lesson."

"I guess so," I replied, having not yet put it together as well as Hal had.

"You speak from the heart, Ted," Hal went on. "And when you speak from the heart, it reaches other people in their hearts."

I looked at Hal, and silently thanked God for such a terrific mentor in my life.

"So guard your heart, Ted," he admonished. "God will continue to use you in a mighty way. Your audiences will continue to be blessed. It's not about hitting them in the head. It's about hitting them in the heart."

THANKS, HAL!

Hal has continued to give me good advice through the years. He and I have maintained a relationship in which I have made myself accountable to him. To this day, we talk to one another two or three times each week. It's an added blessing that his wife, Pamela, is such a good friend to Melanie.

Thanks in no small part to Hal, I'm staying open to the Lord's leading in terms of future ministry. I'm ready, willing, and available. I just want to follow Him.

CURRENT AND FUTURE MINISTRIES

One of the aspects of my life that has taken on real meaning is my involvement with a charity known as the Sunshine Foundation. Based out of Princeton, New Jersey, this organization raises money for terminally ill children. It's very similar to the Make A Wish Foundation, but it was actually started before its more-famous counterpart. The Sunshine Foundation is a great ministry for me because granting the wish of a terminally ill child makes a big difference in the life of someone who is dealing with some of life's most severe circumstances.

I was first invited to participate in the foundation's annual fund-raising dinner at Princeton several years ago. There was a young boy named Rafael who was terminally ill, confined to a wheelchair, and a serious wrestling fan. His wish was to meet the Million Dollar Man, so I was contacted. Once I heard the story, I gladly agreed to be a part of this black-tie affair.

The banquet was a huge success. I met Rafael, and we hit it off terrifically. There were many other kids in attendance, so I spent a good portion of the time hanging out with some of God's most special children. The leadership at the foundation saw how the kids took to me, so they invited me back to take part in the following year's fund-raising activities.

It was such a good match between the foundation and me that after the second year I was invited to become the Goodwill Ambassador for the Sunshine Foundation. I gladly accepted this honor.

This has provided another arm of ministry for me that brings me great joy. The kind folks at the foundation have virtually given me carte blanche in terms of the kids I meet. If I determine a child could be helped by the foundation, I link the two together, and the foundation makes it happen. It is such a wonderful feeling to know these kids are being granted a small amount of joy and fulfillment in the midst of their difficult days.

MY FAMILY

My change from the WWF to the WCW has provided a lot of positive results, not the least of which is that I get to spend more time at home with my family. I can honestly say that Melanie and I have never been happier in our relationship. We have taken up scuba diving together, which has been a real blast! We also have been playing some golf together. I know of marriages that have broken up over chasing the little white ball, but we have made it into a relaxing activity that we enjoy together. (When she starts beating me, we stop keeping score!)

There is also a wonderful sense of teamwork between us as we share together in the responsibility of raising our children. Michael, now nineteen, is a college student at a nearby school. He is playing football on a full scholarship, making good grades, and bringing a sense of pride to Melanie and me.

Now that Michael's in college, he's away from home more, but I feel good that I am there for him when he needs me. We still have some pretty amazing conversations about questions he has on a wide range of issues.

He's playing football, but he also is a fantastic soccer player. Before he graduated, he was chosen as the best goalie in the state of Mississippi in high school soccer. I remember how excited he was to accompany me to Princeton three years ago for the banquet at the Sunshine Foundation. Among the celebrities in attendance was Tony Meola, the goalie for the United States World Cup soccer team. He and Michael hooked up for a lively conversation, which I know is a memory Michael will not soon forget.

That trip is a fond memory for me, as well, but for a different reason altogether. Many people came up to me that evening after meeting Michael and told me how refreshing it was to meet a teenager who is so polite, well-mannered, and respectful to adults.

Michael is a son who makes me very proud.

Of course, I am equally proud of all my boys. Teddy is now fourteen, an athlete, and currently participating in the Olympic Development Program in soccer. It's a real treat for me to be able to make most of his soccer trips and watch him play in his games. Like his older brother, Teddy makes soccer look easy.

But Teddy's special place in our family is his position as the complete out-doorsman. Some of the best memories I have of spending time with him are through the bonding we did while deer hunting. I must admit, I wasn't into it at first, but Teddy won me over to the sport.

Now I'm so hooked on hunting that I've taken steps to incorporate that activity in our lives. For example, I recently sold my car, not because there was anything wrong with it, but in order to buy a brand-new pickup. Now I've got plenty of room to cart home the rewards of our hunting excursions.

Hunting has become such an enjoyable pastime for us that we were recently featured on the television show *Hunting the Country*, which airs on The Nashville Network (TNN). They brought a film crew out to Mississippi to tape Teddy and me on a deer hunt. The producer was thrilled when Teddy bagged a deer right away. "We won't be out here very long!" the producer exclaimed. "Now all we have to do is get Ted on film shooting a deer."

Unfortunately, it wasn't as easy for me. We waited. And waited. And waited. Finally, at dusk, we packed up and headed home, because the crew couldn't film at night. That poor film crew had to come back again. And again.

It was a bit frustrating for all of us, but I continued to assure them that I was just waiting for the right moment, still looking for the Big One! Teddy had a great laugh over this situation, and it brought us closer together as father and son.

Brett is nine and probably the most like his father in terms of his mannerisms and personality. He's a really outgoing, extroverted child, and he can be quite the ham. He's also very active in soccer and baseball, and I'm sure football is in his future. It's such a pleasure to spend time with one of my sons while he is still at such a young age.

GOD'S KIND OF FATHER

Like my dad before me, I have gone to great lengths to warn my boys about their future career choices: "You can grow up to become whatever you want to be…except a professional wrestler!" I tell them. I think they've all heard me loud and clear. But if there were one of the boys who would choose to disobey me and enter the world of wrestling, it would be Brett.

All three of my boys are good students. More significantly, all three of them are very well grounded in their relationship with the Lord. If there's one message they have heard over and over from me, it's this: "Stay close to God!"

I tell them, "If you are ever put in a situation where there's a question about what is right or wrong, think of the Lord Jesus standing right next to you. What would He say? What would He do?" And I also teach my boys that there are repercussions for their actions, which is an important point I want to convey to anyone who reads this book.

Both in good ways and bad ways, my life has demonstrated a key biblical truth: You reap what you sow. My hard work and dedication to my profession paid off in some incredible opportunities that I had during my wrestling career. And good decisions that I've made to follow the Lord and honor my wife have resulted in many blessings and benefits outside the ring as well.

However, when I didn't walk with the Lord, and when I made poor decisions, I reaped negative consequences for myself, and I brought a lot of pain to others who were close to me.

These memories are what make me want to shout, "Stay close to God!"

CONSEQUENCES

Every man has his price. I chose this phrase as the title for this book because it really is more than just a motto I used in my days as the Million Dollar Man. In many ways, it has been a theme of my life. My story illustrates what can happen in a person's life when he or she makes particular choices. A price is paid for every choice we make in our lives.

Kids today want to feel like they are a part of a particular group, so they make certain choices in order to be accepted. But are those choices right? What will the consequences be for the choices that they make?

When my dad died and my mom fell into alcoholism, it would have been very easy for me to shake my fist at God and say, "That's not fair, God! I'll show You. I'll find a way to get back at You!" But to do that would have been to wallow in self-pity and despair and to become consumed by bitterness. I could've chosen to smoke, drink, do drugs, and get into all sorts of trouble, all as ways of getting back at God. After all, I was only a teenager.

But instead, I chose to stay as close to God as possible. I put my focus on positive issues like making the football team, doing the best I could at school, and getting a scholarship at a Division I university. For making the right choices, God rewarded me.

Once I got to college, I made choices that didn't honor the Lord. I lost my focus. I drank. I married at a young age, without knowing what love was or what commitment was all about.

In making those choices, there were consequences. I lost out on knowing my oldest son during his growing-up years. I paid the price of missing out on a possible career in professional football.

Another choice I made was to start college but never finish. I have paid the price for that choice as well. Not having a college degree in today's world is a precarious position to be in. Thankfully, God protected me from injury, or else I could have been devastated financially and been unable to provide for my family.

To this day, it still haunts me that I missed out on my degree by only one year. Only one year.

PAYING THE PRICE

I paid the price to get where I am in my wrestling career. The Bologna Blowouts, the six guys in a cheap motel room, the awful life of a guy on the road all contributed to the price I paid to make it professionally.

I tell young people all the time: "If you set your eyes on Christ, rely on Him as your foundation, ask Him to bless your dreams, and give Him the glory; and if you are willing to do your part, and pay the price it may require, then there's *nothing* that you can't have or do in this world." I have seen it happen over and over in my life and in the lives of others.

But it has to be *your* dream. I can still recall how frustrated some of the guys were who played college football with me. It didn't take long to figure out that college football wasn't their dream. It was the dream of their parents. Most of those guys didn't last very long either.

It goes back to the conversation I had with my dad that summer I wanted to get in shape for football:

"Is this what you really want?" he asked.

"Yes sir."

"Is it coming from your heart?"

"Yes sir."

"Are you going to do this so you can impress others?"

"No sir."

"If you're doing this for any other reason than 'from the heart,' then it's the wrong reason."

"I understand, sir."

"All right, if you really want it for the right reasons, then I will be glad to help you in every way I can."

God says the same thing to all of us.

When Jesus contrasted the wide road that leads to destruction with the narrow road that leads to eternal life, I think He was saying the same thing: Every man has his price. We'll all make the choices that ultimately decide our destiny.

It's up to each one of us.

FOLLOWING GOD'S LEADING

Every person should dream his or her dream and then pursue that dream. As long as it is grounded in the will of God and built on the foundation of Christ, it's the right way to go. If it's not the right way, He will point you in a new direction. It's all about being sensitive to His leading.

I'm learning to follow His direction every day. The Lord has blessed me with a wonderful wife and three great sons. I want to do whatever I can to be the right kind of husband and father in their lives. It's important for us as adults to model positive, Christian values for our kids to follow.

Not long ago, my oldest son, Michael, gave me a card. It wasn't for my birthday or for Christmas. He just wanted to express some feelings he had. I asked him if I could write down his thoughts at the close of the book, and he graciously consented.

The card had a poem on the front about never being alone because of the Lord in our lives. Inside, it simply had printed "Thinking of you and praying for you today." Surrounding the printed message, Michael wrote the following to me:

Dad—I saw this card and it reminded me of the most important thing you have taught me, thus it has already taken me great distances. Dad, I often feel as if I can take on the world simply because I know what is in me! The world cannot accept that I am not afraid—everybody is afraid, but the world doesn't have what we have! I look to you, seeing how I should be; the husband, the father, the caretaker of your family. And I see the only way you do it is through God guiding your every step. You can't go wrong! I see this, Dad! I often think of you and the things you have taught me, and I'm ever so thankful.

You never had what I have now—the father I have in you was gone by this point in your life. But look at yourself, Dad, you've made it—your wife, your kids, the home you live in—you provide for us so very well, by the grace of God.

My desire and drive to achieve the goals I set come from Mike, the one I'm named after. He instilled in you some of the things you've taught me. I know how much you loved him and respected him. The pride you took in naming me after him is instilled in me. Who can stop me if I can become the man you saw in him and the man I see in you, and the man I see in Christ!

I love you, Dad,
Michael

I read this card and just started to cry. I am so thankful for all that has happened in my life. I want to use my life to help others and to serve the Lord. If I can be half the man my son describes in this card, then I will be very fortunate. Indeed, the Lord has brought me a long way.

Thank You, God, for paying the price for a guy like me.

For more information on Ted DiBiase or to arrange a personal appearance, please contact:

Joe Alessi
The Alessi Agency
P. O. Box 10998 #400
Austin, TX 78766

Phone: 512/244-6600
Fax: 512/244-6888
e-mail: alessiagnc@aol.com